Education for

Action

UNDERGRADUATE
AND
GRADUATE PROGRAMS
THAT FOCUS
ON SOCIAL CHANGE

Fourth Edition

Edited by Joan Powell

Food First Books
Oakland, California

We owe a huge debt of gratitude to the many professors whose responses to our inquiries shaped this book. Deepest thanks to all who wrote in with comments and suggestions.

Joan Powell would like to thank Marilyn Borchardt for her particular assistance with the Agriculture section.

Cover design by Colored Horse Studios
Cover photograph by David Bacon
Text design by Harvest Graphics

Library of Congress Cataloging-in-Publication Data

Education for action : undergraduate and graduate programs that focus on social change / edited by Joan Powell. — 4th rev. ed.
    p. cm.
    Includes index.
    ISBN 0-935028-86-2
      1. Social sciences — Study and teaching (Higher) — Directories.
    2. Social change — Study and teaching (Higher) — Directories.
    3. Social sciences — Study and teaching (Higher) — United States —
Directories.   4. Social change — Study and teaching (Higher) —
United States — Directories.   I. Powell, Joan.
    H62.E328 2001
    300'.71'173 — dc21   2001040404

Food First Books are distributed by:

    LPC Group
    1436 West Randolph Street
    Chicago, IL 60607
    (800) 243-0138
    www.coolbooks.com

Printed in Canada

10 9 8 7 6 5 4 3 2 1

TABLE OF CONTENTS

INTRODUCTION

First published in 1987, *Education for Action* provides both graduates and undergraduates with a useful survey of progressive social science programs in higher education.

For this fourth edition, over 250 US academics were canvassed for their recommendations on programs with a progressive orientation or, depending on the discipline, that emphasize social change, sustainable development, public interest issues, heterodox perspectives, or "from-below" approaches to topics. Respondents contributed suggestions with varying degrees of certainty and enthusiasm, ranging from "without doubt one of the best" to "I think they have a few good people" to "progressive students would feel comfortable here." All nominees were carefully reviewed and only those programs with substantial progressive faculty presence and course content were included.

The focus of this book is on schools that offer degrees in the fields covered. This may seem an obvious criterion, but in certain interdisciplinary subjects — area, ethnic, labor, and peace studies, and human rights, for example — the number of actual degree-granting programs is modest to minuscule. No doubt much relevant teaching and scholarship occurs inside these fields yet outside degree tracks, but nearly all nondegree programs were eliminated from this edition in the interests of consistency.

The listings are confined almost exclusively to schools in the United States in order to present options readily accessible to US students. In a few fields — notably education, development studies, and political science — a small handful of schools in Canada and England occurred over and over in the recommendations, so those were included because comparable offerings in this country are sparse. Readers should keep in mind that in most if not all cases, immigration laws in Canada and the UK require international students to present evidence of means to support themselves before they can be admitted to in-country schools. Still, some financial aid is available, and direct Web links to overseas student support offices at each foreign institution are provided. Consult your nearest Canadian or British consulate for more details.

The vast majority of schools described here are universities as opposed to colleges, a disproportion that reflects the responses obtained. A department's reputation is often reinforced through sheer size, research activities, and auxiliary resources, such as institutes, libraries, or affiliated publications, and most colleges cannot compete with universities in these areas. Also, the structure of the book (and the shape of the inquiries sent out) follows disciplinary lines, which favors graduate over undergraduate study. Users of this guide certainly should not assume that only universities offer a quality education to undergraduates interested in progressive viewpoints.

This is not an exhaustive list. Take these ideas as suggestions and opportunities from which to network outward and find other options. Future editions of *Education for Action* will, like this one, rely on the contributions of those presently and formerly within academia, both teachers and students. Please send comments, corrections, and information about programs you think should be included to Food First, Education for Action, 398 60th Street, Oakland, California 94618.

AGRICULTURE

Iowa State University
Graduate Program in Sustainable Agriculture
110 Curtiss Hall
Ames, IA 50011-1050
Phone: 515-294-6061
Email: *gpsa@iastate.edu*
Web site: *www.sust.ag.iastate.edu/gpsa/*
Degrees: M.S., Ph.D.

The newly inaugurated Graduate Program in Sustainable Agriculture (GPSA) at Iowa State University draws on the expertise of fifty faculty members in ten academic departments. The intent of the program is to develop student competence and expertise in the design, implementation, and evaluation of sustainable agricultural systems. Prescribed courses are minimal in number; it is the prerogative of students, in consultation with their advisory committees, to develop programs of study tailored to their needs and interests. Master's students should have a bachelor's degree and a strong record of achievement in one of the natural sciences, social sciences, or engineering sciences, or a bachelor's degree plus equivalent experience in these areas. Ph.D. students must have a master's degree and either an undergraduate or master's degree in one of the majors in the College of Agriculture or its equivalent.

Iowa State offers a wealth of institutes, extension programs, and experiential learning opportunities concerned with the study and practice of sustainable agriculture. Its student-operated organic farm grows produce for local outlets, including a community-supported agriculture system.

COURSE HIGHLIGHTS: Pesticides in the Environment/Theory of Public Goods and Externalities/Restoration Ecology/ Environmental Bioprocessing of Agricultural Byproducts/

Technological Innovation, Social Change, and Development/
Contaminant Hydrogeology.

SELECTED FACULTY

Lorna Michael Butler: Urban agriculture, participatory research,
entrepreneurial agriculture, minority roles in sustainable
agriculture, global issues in sustainability.
Clare Hinrichs: Direct agricultural markets, community food
security, regionality and quality in food supply chains, multi-
functionality in agricultural systems.
Hsain Ilahiane: Natural and cultural resource management,
agricultural and technological change, ethnic stratification, arid
land ecology and development.
Matt Liebman: Crop rotation, intercropping, and cover cropping
systems; weed ecology and management.
John Sandor: Impacts of agriculture on soils and landscapes, soils
and agricultural archaeology, indigenous knowledge of soils.

University of Maine
Sustainable Agriculture Program
5722 Deering Hall
Orono, ME 04469-5722
Phone: 207-581-2913
Fax: 207-581-2999
Email: *mariann2@maine.edu*
Web site: *www.umaine.edu/pse/sag.htm*
Degree: B.S.

The University of Maine offers academic, research, and extension
programs in sustainable agriculture addressing the principles and
practices of environmentally sound and profitable farming. The
undergraduate academic program covers how to increase farm
profits by decreasing the costs of crop and livestock production;
how to build soil tilth and fertility through rotations, multiple
cropping, and nutrient cycling; how to protect water quality by
decreasing the need to use synthetic agrichemicals; how to man-

age crop pests and livestock diseases with integrated, ecologically sound strategies; and how to create a strong, diversified agriculture that is stable through market and weather fluctuations. The Sustainable Agriculture Bachelor of Science is an interdisciplinary program offered cooperatively by the faculties of the Departments of Plant, Soil, and Environmental Sciences; Plant Biology and Pathology; and Resource Economics and Policy. In addition to the core courses, students obtain knowledge and skills in the liberal arts, mathematics, sciences, and communications.

COURSE HIGHLIGHTS: Sustainable Development and Public Policy/Agricultural Pest Ecology/Soil Organic Matter and Fertility/ Pesticides and the Environment/Weed Ecology and Management/ Plant Pathology/Crop Ecology and Physiology/Cropping Systems.

SELECTED FACULTY

M. Susan Erich: Composition of crop residues, roots and organic residuals in soils.
Dave Lambert: Ecology, management, and control of crop diseases.
Gregory Porter: Improved soil management as an alternative to supplemental irrigation, crop responses to cultural practices.
Marianne Sarrantonio: Cover cropping and soil nitrogen conservation.

Also recommended

University of California, Santa Cruz
Center for Agroecology and Sustainable Food Systems
1156 High Street
Santa Cruz, CA 95064
Phone: 831-459-3240
Fax: 831-459-2799
Web site: *zzyx.ucsc.edu/casfs/*

The Center for Agroecology and Sustainable Food Systems at the University of California, Santa Cruz is a research, education, and

public service program dedicated to increasing ecological sustainability and social justice in the food and agriculture system. The
Center serves as a resource for graduate and undergraduate students interested in sustainable agriculture, agricultural policy,
food security, rural studies, and related topics. Undergraduates
and doctoral students in the university's Environmental Studies
Department can pursue agroecology and sustainable agriculture
as an area of emphasis within their respective degree programs.

ANTHROPOLOGY

University of California, Berkeley
Department of Anthropology
232 Kroeber Hall
Berkeley, CA 94720-3710
Phone: 510-642-3391
Fax: 510-643-8557
Email: *anthapp@uclink.berkeley.edu*
Web site: *ls.berkeley.edu/dept/anth/*
Degrees: B.A., M.A., Ph.D.

The Department of Anthropology at the University of California,
Berkeley is among the foremost departments in the United States,
a position it has held for decades. The department offers a Ph.D. in
anthropology within the sub-disciplines of social cultural anthropology or archaeology. In the first year of the program, the student
attends lectures and seminars and defines his or her topical and
geographical specialization. During the second year and the beginning of the third year, students elect other seminars, courses, or
language training as appropriate to individualized plans of study.
Several of these courses must be chosen from a core curriculum of

advanced pro-seminars covering theory, practice, and method in different fields. The seminars and individual research work during this period are directed toward preparing the student's three field statements and fulfilling the language requirement, necessary in the preparation for the Ph.D. oral qualifying examination. In cooperation with the University of California, San Francisco, the department offers a Ph.D. in medical anthropology. A Master of Arts in folklore is also available.

Twelve courses are required for the Bachelor of Arts degree. The department offers several types of independent study opportunities for undergraduates whereby academic credit may be earned for fieldwork, internships, specialized group study, or independent research projects.

COURSE HIGHLIGHTS: Globalization, Governmentality, and Citizenship/Ethnographies of the State/Orientalism, Occidentalisms, and Control/Cultures of Post-Socialism/Time, Narrative, and Ethnography/Tribal Society/Public Archaeology/ China: A History of the Future.

SELECTED FACULTY

Gerald Berreman: Social inequality, interaction theory, research methods and ethics, urban society, small-scale societies, India, Himalayas, Arctic.

Laura Nader: Comparative ethnography of law and dispute resolution, comparative family organizations, ethnology of the Middle East, Mexico, Latin America, US.

Aihwa Ong: Political economy, gender and sexuality, colonialism, nationalism, transnationalism, citizenship and US Asian immigrants, Southeast Asia, South China.

Nancy Scheper-Hughes: Critical medical anthropology, the anthropology of violence, madness and culture, inequality and marginality, Ireland, Brazil, Cuba, South Africa.

University of Chicago
Department of Anthropology
1126 East 59th Street
Chicago, IL 60637
Phone: 773-702-8551
Fax: 773-702-4503
Email: *anthro@anthro.spc.uchicago.edu*
Web site: *anthropology.uchicago.edu/index.html*
Degrees: B.A., Ph.D.

The Department of Anthropology at the University of Chicago offers doctoral programs in archaeology and in sociocultural and linguistic anthropology. Although doctoral students must complete an M.A. paper during their course of study (or receive credit for an M.A. degree earned at another institution), no one is admitted to the department solely to seek an M.A.; terminal M.A. degrees are granted at the discretion of the department. Some of the areas that are currently enjoying particular attention by faculty and students in the department include semiotic approaches to culture, post-colonialism, human rights and indigenous rights, globalization, critiques of neoliberalism, the politics of gender and sexuality, the analysis of place and space, and the anthropological study of science. Graduate students collaborate with faculty on a host of research projects and workshops.

The Bachelor of Arts program in anthropology consists of thirteen courses; at least ten are normally chosen from those listed or cross-listed as Department of Anthropology courses. A special honors program is open to outstanding students with an overall grade point average of 3.25 or better who wish to develop an extended piece of research through a bachelor's essay under the approved supervision of a faculty member.

COURSE HIGHLIGHTS: Political Subjectivity: Power, Fantasy, and the Real/Indigenous Intellectual Rights/Anthropology of Development/Colonialism–Post Colonialism: The Dialectics of Modernity/Intellectual Culture in Modern China: Knowledge,

Power, and Criticism/Migrancy and Social Reproduction in Rural South Africa.

SELECTED FACULTY

Arjun Appadurai: Sociocultural anthropology, globalization, public culture, South Asia.

Manuela Carneiro da Cunha: Indigenous history, rights, and knowledge; Amazonian ethnology; conservation and traditional peoples; slavery and emancipation; Brazil.

John L. Comaroff: Political and legal systems, historical anthropology, colonialism and post-colonialism, modernity and the politics of identity, Africa.

Elizabeth Povinelli: Language, culture, and power; sexuality and gender; indigenous and human rights; colonial/postcolonial studies; Australia/Oceania; US.

Michel-Rolph Trouillot: Historicity, power, the Caribbean.

City University of New York Graduate Center

Ph.D. Program in Anthropology
365 Fifth Avenue
New York, NY 10016
Phone: 212-817-8005
Fax: 212-817-1501
Email: *anthropology@gc.cuny.edu*
Web site: *web.gc.cuny.edu/Anthropology/home.html*
Degree: Ph.D.

The Ph.D. Program in Anthropology at CUNY Graduate Center provides doctoral training in each of the discipline's sub-fields: cultural anthropology, archaeology, physical anthropology, and linguistic anthropology. The program is committed to excellence in training its students for careers in research and teaching as well as nonacademic fields. In addition to coursework, students have opportunities for early fieldwork experience through faculty-directed practicums and summer research funding. A minimum of 60 credits of approved coursework is required for the Ph.D.

Students design their courses of study in consultation with an advisor. The first level provides grounding in general anthropology, theory, and the basic concepts and methods of the student's sub-field. At the second level, students pursue advanced work within the sub-field, selected from the broad range of specialties represented on the faculty. The third level, after completion of 60 credits, is devoted to research for the dissertation. Students must pass written and oral examinations, demonstrate language proficiency, and submit a research proposal before advancement to candidacy.

For students interested in undergraduate and/or master's work in anthropology, CUNY's Hunter College offers an outstanding program.

COURSE HIGHLIGHTS: Political Economy of Urbanization/ Social Science and the African Diaspora/Seminar in Nationalism and Ethnicity/Seminar in Place, Culture, and Politics/Foundations of Anthropological Thought: Marx, Weber, Durkheim.

SELECTED FACULTY
Uradyn Bulag: Mongolian political culture and nationalism, Chinese colonialism, nationalism and politics of culture in multiethnic states.
Marc Edelman: Economic and political anthropology, historical anthropology, Latin America.
David Harvey: Human geography, urban studies, global flow of capital.
Joan Mencher: Socioeconomic development, gender, sustainable agricultural systems, South Asia.
Leith Mullings: Globalization, urbanism, medical anthropology, gender, race, ethnicity, contemporary theory, US urban populations, Africa.

University of Massachusetts, Amherst
Department of Anthropology
Box 34805

Machmer Hall
University of Massachusetts
Amherst, MA 01003-4805
Phone: 413-545-2221
Fax: 413-545-9494
Email (graduate): *oriol@anthro.umass.edu*
Email (undergraduate): *sbellor@anthro.umass.edu*
Web site: *www.umass.edu/anthro*
Degrees: B.A., M.A., Ph.D.

The Department of Anthropology at the University of Massachusetts, Amherst emphasizes broad knowledge in four sub-fields of the discipline: archaeology, cultural or social anthropology, linguistic anthropology, and biological anthropology. In choosing courses and in selecting topics both for statements of field and for the thesis and dissertation, students will find the faculty, particularly their faculty committees, encouraging the development of breadth as well as particular skill in a chosen sub-field. Students in this program can expect to be regularly asked about the relevance of their work for practitioners in other sub-fields. Students in the M.A. program complete a personal curriculum of courses and assignments developed in consultation with a faculty advisory committee. Most students also write and defend a master's thesis. Soon after entry into the Ph.D. program, the student, in consultation with a faculty guidance committee, designates three fields of specialization that reflect his or her career goals and intellectual interests. Doctoral candidates prepare and present a prospectus in a departmental seminar and pass an oral comprehensive exam before embarking on the dissertation.

Anthropology majors complete a minimum of 36 credits in the field, including at least one course in each of the four sub-fields, a junior-year writing sequence, a methods course in research design and statistical analysis, and a hands-on research course. Students in the honors program take honors courses and submit a thesis.

COURSE HIGHLIGHTS: Anthropology in the Public Interest/
Andean Archaeology and Ethnohistory/Comparative Social
Systems/Revolution and Social Change/Anthropology of
Communication/Contemporary Anthropological Theory.

SELECTED FACULTY

Ralph Faulkingham: Demographic and socioeconomic change
in rural development, political economy of colonialism and
development, Africa.

Oriol Pi-Sunyer: Political and economic anthropology, the
modern state, minority nationalism, tourism, maritime
anthropology, Europe, Mesoamerica.

R. Brooke Thomas: Human adaptability and political ecology,
biocultural processes of change in mountain areas, effects of
tourism, Andes, Yucatan, New England.

Jacqueline Urla: Ethnicity, gender, and sexuality; linguistic
anthropology; visual anthropology; Western Europe; Spain.

Michigan State University
Department of Anthropology
354 Baker Hall
East Lansing, MI 48824
Phone: 517-353-2950
Fax: 517-432-2363
Email: *barrickl@msu.edu*
Web site: *www.ssc.msu.edu/~anp/*
Degrees: B.A., B.S., M.A., Ph.D.

The Department of Anthropology at Michigan State University
offers the M.A. and Ph.D. degrees in anthropology. Most students
earn the M.A. degree while continuing their studies toward the
doctorate, although it is possible to complete only the M.A.
degree. The faculty represents all four traditional sub-fields, with
particular expertise in Africa, Asia, Latin America, and North
American culture and prehistory. Within these geographic areas,
the department has programmatic emphases in the study of cul-

ture, resources, and power; medical anthropology; forensic anthropology and skeletal biology; and Great Lakes ethnohistory and archaeology. In addition, the faculty's broader interests span sub-field boundaries to include the study of agriculture and the environment, social inequality and social institutions, public policy and cultural impact assessment, systems of communication and meaning, and medical and legal issues.

For either the B.A. or B.S. degree, students must complete a minimum of thirty credits in anthropology, including two introductory-level classes, one culture-area course, one thematic or analytical course, and five electives, three of which must be at the 300 level or above. A departmental writing-intensive capstone course rounds out the major. Outstanding students may apply for admission to MSU's Honors College, which offers an individualized and accelerated four-year program.

COURSE HIGHLIGHTS: Frontiers and Colonization in Historical Archaeology/Environments of International Enterprise/Gender Relations in Comparative Perspective/Food, Hunger, and Society/ Culture, Resources, and Power/Urban Anthropology.

SELECTED FACULTY

William Derman: Social structure and social change in peasant societies, social impact analysis and development planning.
Anne Ferguson: Southern Africa, agrarian and environmental change, social impact analysis, gender relations.
Susan Krouse: Urban American Indian communities.
Ann Millard: Health inequality, bicultural approaches to population dynamics and nutrition, cultural history of biomedicine.

Stanford University
Department of Cultural and Social Anthropology
Building 110, Room 111-D1 (Main Quad)
Stanford, CA 94305-2145
Phone: 650-723-3421

Fax: 650-725-0605
Email: *cultural.social.anthro@stanford.edu*
Web site: *www.stanford.edu/dept/cultsoc-anthro/*
Degrees: A.B., M.A., Ph.D.

The Department of Cultural and Social Anthropology (CASA) at Stanford University offers programs both for students who seek the Ph.D. degree and for those who seek the master's degree only. Entering graduate students need not have majored in anthropology as undergraduates, although most have backgrounds in behavioral sciences. Students are free to specialize in a variety of fields and to develop programs that fit their own research interests. The faculty consists of leading contributors to our understanding of ethnic, sub-national, religious, and linguistic conflict in different parts of the world. Research commitments include the study of nationalism and sub-nationalism, religion, mass media, kinship, gender, feminism, ethnicity and race, material culture, medical anthropology, relations between communities and states, and transnational cultural flows.

The department offers an A.B. degree in Cultural and Social Anthropology, an undergraduate minor, and department honors. A program of 65 units, with at least 40 units in the discipline, is required. Students must choose a concentration and develop competence in a foreign language beyond first-year level.

COURSE HIGHLIGHTS: Archaeology and Globalism/Tourism, Heritage, and National Identity/Millennialism in the American Imaginary/Sex, Blood, and Representation/Theories of the Postcolonial/The Multicultural City in Europe/Naturalizing Power.

SELECTED FACULTY

Carol Delaney: Cultural anthropology, gender, religion, Mediterranean, Middle East, Turkey.
Paulla Ebron: Comparative cultural studies, nationalism, gender, discourses of identity, Africa, African America.

Akhil Gupta: Political economy, ethnography of the state, discourse of development, peasants, bureaucracies, applied anthropology, Marxism, South Asia.
Renato Rosaldo: History and society, island Southeast Asia, US Latinos and Latin America.

University of Texas
Department of Anthropology
Austin, TX 78712-1086
Phone: 512-471-4206
Fax: 512-471-6535
Email (undergraduate): *sosbakken@mail.utexas.edu*
Email (graduate): *neathery@mail.utexas.edu*
Web site: *www.utexas.edu/cola/depts/anthropology/*
Degrees: B.A, M.A., Ph.D.

The Department of Anthropology at the University of Texas grants the B.A., M.A., and Ph.D. degrees, and offers programs in social, linguistic, and physical anthropology, archaeology, and folklore. Graduate specializations in African diaspora and Mexican borderlands studies are available. The faculty teaches in most areas of geographical interest, with particular strength in the native populations of North, Central, and South America. The school encourages interdisciplinary study and provides numerous opportunities for fieldwork. The M.A. degree requires a minimum of 30 semester hours of credit, including six hours in a related minor subject, and a thesis or a report that has been approved by the department and the graduate school. Of the 30 hours, 24 are normally in regular courses and six are represented by the preparation of the thesis. At the Ph.D. level, each student is expected to acquire basic competence in at least four of the five sub-areas of anthropology, demonstrate reading proficiency in a foreign language, and pass the written qualifying examination before proceeding to the dissertation.

Students enrolled in the graduate program have the opportunity to pursue a track in activist anthropology. This track has three components: a sequence of preparatory courses, an activist research internship lasting six months or longer, and a master's report or thesis based on the internship experience. "Activist anthropology" refers to research, writing, and teaching that are directly involved with the efforts of communities, organizations, movements, or networks to analyze the root causes of inequality, oppression, conflict, and violence; to formulate strategies to transform these conditions; and to achieve the power necessary to make these strategies effective. The program builds on the best of a long tradition of the creative combination of scholarship and social activism within the discipline, while at the same time encouraging critical reflection on both the conceptual and practical limitations of that tradition.

COURSE HIGHLIGHTS: Transnationalism: Case Studies and Theories/Theories of Social Control and Confinement/Race, Resistance, and Urban Politics/Oral Traditions and History/ Theory, Practice, and Politics of Fieldwork.

SELECTED FACULTY

Begona Aretxaga: Ethnicity, gender, political violence, colonialism and nationalism, Europe.
Edmund Gordon: African American anthropology, economic anthropology, maritime anthropology, ethnicity and social stratification, the Caribbean and Central America.
Charles Hale: Indigenous movements, ethnic and racial politics, nationalism and state-society relations, Mesoamerican people and histories.
Kamala Visweswaran: Social anthropology, feminist theory and ethnography, critical historiography, nationalism, South Asia.

Also recommended:

American University
Department of Anthropology
4400 Massachusetts Avenue, NW
Washington, DC 20016
Phone: 202-885-1830

Email: *anthro@american.edu*
Web site: *www.american.edu/academic.depts/cas/anthro*
Degrees: B.A., M.A., Ph.D.

Graduate fields of specialization, Ph.D.: Urban anthropology; ethnicity; the anthropology of work; the anthropology of development; language, culture, and cognition; gender and culture; cross-cultural quantitative analysis; historic and public archaeology.

Graduate fields of specialization, M.A.: Cross-cultural research, urban studies, cultural dynamics and change, ethnicity, gender studies, linguistic analysis, cultural resources management, public archaeology, anthropology of development, anthropology of education, applied linguistics.

New School University
Graduate Faculty of Political and Social Science
Department of Anthropology
Room 320
65 Fifth Avenue
New York, NY 10003
Phone: 212-229-5757
Fax: 212-229-5595
Web site: *www.newschool.edu/gf/anthro/index.htm*
Degrees: B.A., M.A., Ph.D., D.S.Sc.

Three thematic concentrations: Cultural theory; gender; anthropology and history.

AREA STUDIES–AFRICA

Binghamton University
Department of Africana Studies
Box 6000
Binghamton, NY 13902-6000
Phone: 607-777-2635
Fax: 607-777-6547
Email: *bkumiega@binghamton.edu*
Web site: *africana.binghamton.edu*
Degree: B.A.

The Africana Studies Department at Binghamton University focuses both on African peoples and cultures and on New World peoples of African descent. The department's curriculum ranges across traditional fields of anthropology, art history, history, literature, political science, sociology, theater, and other disciplines; several of its faculty hold joint appointments in other departments. Courses approach subject matter from a non-Eurocentric and nonracial perspective and broaden those disciplines in which the knowledge of the presence, contributions, and experiences of African people and their descendants have been omitted or neglected. For the major, eight courses (32 credits) taken within the department are required. Many students choose to pursue double majors with one of the related departments represented in Africana studies. An honors option requiring a thesis is available.

COURSE HIGHLIGHTS: West African History, 16th to 20th Century/African Women and Feminism/Islam and the West/Cultural Forces in World Politics/Politics, Race, and Representation in the US/Economics of International Institutions/Black Families.

SELECTED FACULTY

Ricardo Laremont: Nationalism, peacekeeping, and war in Africa; political Islam.

Nkiru Nzegwu: Gender and feminism in Africa and African studies, African art history.

Darryl Thomas: North-South relations, international relations of Africa, globalization and state fragmentation, comparative Black politics and political thought, urban politics.

Cynthia Young: Cultural theory, US radical culture, Black popular culture, literature of the diaspora.

University of California, Los Angeles

James S. Coleman African Studies Center
10244 Bunche Hall
405 Hilgard Avenue
Los Angeles, CA 90095-1310
Phone: 310-825-3686
Fax: 310-206-2250
Email: *jscasc@isop.ucla.edu*
Web site: *www.isop.ucla.edu/jscasc*
Degree: M.A.

Originally established in 1959, the James S. Coleman African Studies Center at UCLA supports and promotes academic, research, and outreach programs on Africa and has been designated a National Resource Center for African Studies. The Center offers an interdepartmental Master of Arts in African area studies. Fulfillment of an indigenous language requirement and completion of a minimum of nine courses (36 units) are required for the master's degree. Students may satisfy their final degree requirement by writing a master's thesis or by taking a comprehensive examination. While there is no Ph.D. program in African studies at UCLA, students can apply to and enroll in Ph.D. programs in other disciplines and choose to focus their research on Africa. Undergraduates may earn a certificate in the field; this specialization can be taken only jointly

with work towards a bachelor's degree, normally in one of the following fields: anthropology, economics, geography, history, linguistics, political science, or sociology.

COURSE HIGHLIGHTS: Comparative Systems of Social
Inequality/Problems of Underdeveloped Countries/Africa in the
Age of Imperialism/Ideology and the Developing World/The
Role of Intelligence Agencies in Africa/Seminar in Political Change.

SELECTED FACULTY

Judith Carney: African environmental knowledge systems in the
Americas; women and water rights in irrigation development;
culture, technology, and the environment.
Sondra Hale: Gender, political economy, social movements,
postcolonial and cultural studies, Middle East and Africa.
Gail Harrison: International health and nutrition, pediatric and
maternal nutrition.
Edmond Keller: African development and public policy, political
transitions in Africa, African regional security issues, democracy
and human rights.
William Worger: Social and economic history of southern Africa.

University of Illinois, Urbana-Champaign

Center for African Studies
210 International Studies Building
910 South Fifth Street
Champaign, IL 61820
Phone: 217-333-6335
Fax: 217-244-2429
Email: *african@uiuc.edu*
Web site: *www.afrst.uiuc.edu*
Degree: M.A.

The Center for African Studies at the University of Illinois, Urbana-
Champaign offers a Master of Arts in African studies. More than
thirty faculty members whose teaching and research are signifi-

cantly related to Africa constitute the core faculty. The master's in African studies requires successful completion of 8.5 units of approved graduate course work from at least three disciplines and proficiency (equivalent to six semesters of study) in an indigenous African language. Courses taken to fulfill the language proficiency requirement are not credited towards the 8.5 units. Approved courses usually are devoted entirely to Africa or African studies in their content. Students may pursue a thesis option if a member of the core faculty agrees to serve as an advisor, guiding research conducted during independent study. Master's students are expected to take an active part in the life of the Center; regular activities include a weekly seminar, spring symposium, and numerous guest speakers. An undergraduate minor is also available.

COURSE HIGHLIGHTS: Pan-Africanism in the Americas, Europe, and Africa/Comparative Environmental History: People, Crops, and Capital/Kinship and Social Organization in Africa/Mashrek and Mahgreb Literature of French Expression/Egypt since the First World War/Race, Gender, and Class in South Africa 1880 to Present.

SELECTED FACULTY

Merle Bowen: Comparative politics, government and politics in developing countries, African politics, rural development policy.
Mahir Saul: Colonial period in West Africa; Islam, Catholic missions, local shrines; agrarian development and ecology.
Gale Summerfield: Gender and development, economic development, environmental-resource economics, international economics.
Paul Tiyambe Zeleza: African economic history of the 19th and 20th centuries, production of knowledge in Africa, democratic transformation in Africa.

Also recommended

Michigan State University
African Studies Center

100 Center for International Programs
East Lansing, MI 48824-1035
Phone: 517-353-1700
Fax: 517-432-1209
Email: *africa@msu.edu*
Web site: *www.isp.msu.edu/africanstudies*

The African Studies Center at Michigan State University has been designated an African Foreign Language and Area Studies Center by the US Department of Education, from which it receives partial funding. The Center offers an undergraduate specialization and a graduate certificate in African studies.

AREA STUDIES–ASIA

Cornell University
Mario Einaudi Center for International Studies
170 Uris Hall
Ithaca, NY 14853
Phone: 607-255-6370
Fax: 607-254-5000
Email: *einaudi_center@admin.is.cornell.edu*
Web site: *www.einaudi.cornell.edu*
Degrees: B.A., M.A.

The Mario Einaudi Center for International Studies serves as the umbrella organization and provides financial and logistical support for more than twenty programs in area, thematic, and development studies at Cornell University. Its programs in East Asian, South Asian, and Southeast Asian studies are among the most comprehensive in the country. Students may earn a Bachelor of Arts or Master of Arts degree in Asian studies with concentrations in any of the three programs. Asian languages currently taught at Cornell are Bengali, Burmese, Cambodian, Cebuano, Chinese (Mandarin and Cantonese), Hindi-Urdu, Indonesian, Japanese, Javanese, Korean, Pali, Sanskrit, Sinhalese, Tagalog, Tamil, Thai, and Vietnamese. For M.A. candidates, a minimum of two semesters in residence at Cornell is required; more than two may be necessary for students lacking background in language study. Students must demonstrate oral and written proficiency in a language relevant to their concentration equivalent to three years of non-intensive study and submit a thesis of thirty to fifty pages in length. The undergraduate major consists of 36 credits in Asian studies, including six in a relevant language and 18 in the chosen area of concentration.

COURSE HIGHLIGHTS: Virtual Orientalisms/China and the West Before Imperialism/The Plural Society Revisited/Gender and Sexuality in Southeast Asian History/Constructing Shangri-La: Writing About Tibet/Crisis Cults, Millenarian Movements, and New Religions in Japan.

SELECTED FACULTY

Ben Anderson: Nationalism and militarism in a world context, political culture and comparative colonialism in Southeast Asia.
Paul Gellert: Southeast Asia, sociology of natural resources and development, political sociology, comparative and historical methods.
Victor Koschmann: Modern Japanese history.
Tamara Loos: Gender studies and law in Thai history.
Kathryn March: Gender, identity, and change, specifically in the Nepal Himalaya.

Also recommended

University of Michigan
Center for Chinese Studies
Web site: *www.umich.edu/~iinet/ccs*
Center for Japanese Studies

Web site: *www.umich.edu/~iinet/cjs*
Center for South and Southeast Asian Studies
Web site: *www.umich.edu/~iinet/csseas*
Degree: M.A.

At the University of Michigan, area centers in Chinese, Japanese, and South and Southeast Asian studies offer interdisciplinary M.A. degrees. These centers are independently administered and separate from the university's language- and humanities-oriented B.A. and Ph.D. programs. Each maintains different contact information and degree requirements.

AREA STUDIES–LATIN AMERICA

University of Arizona
Latin American Area Center
103 Douglass Building
Tucson, AZ 85716
Phone: 520-626-7242
Fax: 520-626-7248
Email: *laac@u.arizona.edu*
Web site: *las.arizona.edu*
Degrees: B.A., M.A.

The Latin American Area Center at the University of Arizona administers the school's Latin American studies program and coordinates a broad range of instructional, research, and outreach activities relating to Latin America. The program offers B.A. and M.A. degrees and a Ph.D. minor. Faculty research and teaching strengths include Mexico, Brazil, environmental studies, border studies, indigenous studies, and women's studies. Coursework for the interdisciplinary M.A. comprises two fields of study, a core Latin American studies research seminar, and optional electives. Because of the interdisciplinary nature and regional emphasis of the master's program, both Spanish and Portuguese skills are required. The fields of study available for areas of primary concentration are anthropology, geography and regional development, history, political science, Spanish and Portuguese, and women's studies. Master's candidates choose one of three exam options: a thesis defense, a comprehensive oral exam, or a combination written and oral exam. The writing of a thesis is strongly encouraged.

Students majoring in Latin American studies must complete a minimum of 30 upper-division units. At least 12 of these must come from a concentration in one of the following areas: anthropology, art history, geography and regional development, history, political science, Portuguese, or Spanish.

COURSE HIGHLIGHTS: In the Wake of the Green Revolution/ Democracies, Emerging and Evolving/The US-Mexican Borderlands in Comparative Perspective/Latin America and the Global Economy: Markets, Governments, and Civil Society/US Counter-Narcotics Policy in Latin America.

SELECTED FACULTY

Ana Alonso: Sociocultural and historical anthropology; culture and power; ethnography as a genre; gender, ethnicity, and class; colonial and post-colonial societies; nationalism.

James Anaya: International law and organization, with emphasis on issues of self-determination and the rights of indigenous peoples.

Kevin Gosner: Colonial Latin America, Mayan ethnohistory, southern Mexico and Guatemala, peasants and agrarian revolt.

Maria Carmen Lemos: Public policy-making in Latin America with a focus on Brazil and Mexico, social movements and popular participation in urban environmental policy-making.

Raúl Saba: Latin American political development, informal economy, Peruvian politics.

University of Wisconsin
Latin American, Caribbean, and Iberian Studies Program
209 Ingraham Hall
1155 Observatory Drive
Madison, WI 53706
Phone: 608-262-2811
Fax: 608-265-5851
Email (undergraduate): *wney@lss.wisc.edu*
Email (graduate): *latam@macc.wisc.edu*
Web site: *polyglot.lss.wisc.edu/laisp*
Degrees: B.A., M.A.

The University of Wisconsin's Latin American, Caribbean, and Iberian Studies program (LACIS) offers the B.A., M.A., and Ph.D. minor. It also coordinates outreach activities and administers an internship/research initiative with a network of nonprofit organizations working on or in Latin America. The Master of Arts degree is designed to facilitate interdisciplinary study of Latin America, Spain, and Portugal. Aside from a core seminar on trends in Latin American studies, the program has no courses of its own and no separate course listing in the timetable. Rather, students take courses from an array of departments that have offerings relevant to the field; these include, among others, agriculture, anthropology, business, economics, geography, history, journalism, law, political science, sociology, Spanish, Portuguese, and Quechua. Completion of the degree requires 24 credits of courses with Latin American and Iberian language and area content, consisting of 12 credits in a field of concentration and 12 credits in one or more other fields. Certification of basic proficiency in Spanish or Portuguese and satisfactory performance in a one-hour oral examination are also required.

The major in Latin American, Caribbean, and Iberian studies

provides broad exposure to the field through area content courses in several disciplines, concentrated training in one group of academic disciplines, and basic working knowledge of Spanish and/or Portuguese. A minimum of 40 credits is required for the LACIS major.

COURSE HIGHLIGHTS: Revolution and Conflict in Modern Latin America/Colony, Nation, and Minority: The Puerto Rican's World/Mass Communication, Culture, and Human Rights/ Challenge of Democratization/Political Violence and Memory/ Income Distribution and Social Exclusion.

SELECTED FACULTY
Jane Collins: Formal and informal sector labor in agriculture, gender and labor process, international division of labor, feminist theory, cultural theory.
Leigh Payne: Latin American politics, Brazil, women, democratic consolidation.
Steve Stern: Amerindian responses to colonialism, gender relations, political economy, social acquiescence and rebelliousness, memories of trauma and political violence.
Karl Zimmerer: Geography of Latin America, agriculture and rural land use in peasant and indigenous societies, development and tropical environments.

Also recommended

Indiana University
Center for Latin American and Caribbean Studies
1125 East Atwater Avenue
Bloomington, IN 47401
Phone: 812-855-9097
Fax: 812-855-5345
Email: *clacs@indiana.edu*
Web site: *www.indiana.edu/~clacs*
Degree: M.A.

The Center for Latin American and Caribbean Studies draws upon distinguished faculty in the humanities, social sciences, fine arts, and a number of professional programs. It offers a Master of Arts degree and both undergraduate and Ph.D. certificates and minors.

AREA STUDIES–MIDDLE EAST

New York University
Hagop Kevorkian Center
50 Washington Square South
New York, NY 10012
Phone: 212-998-8877
Fax: 212-995-4144
Email: *kevorkian.center@nyu.edu*
Web site: *www.nyu.edu/gsas/program/nearest*
Degrees: B.A., M.A., Ph.D.

The Hagop Kevorkian Center for Near Eastern Studies at New York University is an area studies center, funded in part by the federal government, whose mission is to encourage and coordinate teaching and research on the Middle East at NYU and to sponsor educational, informational, and outreach programs for teachers, the general public, and other people interested in the region. It offers an M.A. program in modern Middle Eastern studies and joint M.A. programs that combine the study of the Middle East with Journalism, Museum Studies, and Business. The Center cooperates closely with the Department of Middle Eastern Studies, which offers separate programs of study leading to the B.A. and Ph.D. degrees. The M.A. program is designed for those thinking of entering a Ph.D. program but wanting first to explore different disciplines or advance their knowledge of the region and its languages; and for those planning a career in fields such as journalism, public service, cultural organizations, human rights, or political advocacy and seeking to understand the region's politics and history and to engage with questions of culture, social transformation, and economic justice.

COURSE HIGHLIGHTS: The Crusades: A Reevaluation/Women and Islamic Law/Jerusalem: The Contested Inheritance/Financial Markets of the Arabian Gulf/Reporting the Middle East/Communities of Knowledge: Medieval Histories and Identities/Ottoman Socioeconomic History.

SELECTED FACULTY

Shiva Balaghi: Iranian cultural history, gender studies, history of colonialism and nationalism in the Middle East.

Michael Gilsenan: Anthropology of Arab societies, urban studies, forms of power and hierarchy.

Zachary Lockman: Modern Middle Eastern history, especially Egypt and Palestine; Middle East labor and sociocultural history.

Samer Shehata: Political economy of development, labor and working class history, social theory, comparative politics of the Middle East, Middle Eastern ethnography.

DEVELOPMENT STUDIES

American University
International Development Program
School of International Service
4400 Massachusetts Avenue NW
Washington, DC 20016-8071
Phone: 202-885-1660

Fax: 202-885-1695
Email: *idpsis@american.edu*
Web site: *american.edu/sis/fields/id*
Degrees: M.A., M.S.

The International Development Program at American University's School of International Service offers two master's degrees. Both degrees combine theory and practice, are anchored by a required multidisciplinary core, and students can select a particular focus of concentration. The M.A. in international development provides a multidisciplinary overview of development issues and policies, enabling students to focus on a particular field of concentration. The M.S. in development management offers more focused training to individuals with experience working on development projects; it combines skills from development and public administration for those specifically interested in management of development activities. Students in this practice-oriented program are afforded an opportunity to focus on innovative approaches to development management that are presently being used both in the United States and in the Third World, with particular attention to the issues of self-reliance, sustainability, and poverty alleviation.

Students in American University's highly competitive Ph.D. program in international studies may elect international development as a Ph.D major field.

COURSE HIGHLIGHTS: Class and Culture/Thinking Beyond Globalization/NGOs and International Development/ Micropolitics of Development/Development Finance and Banking/Nonformal Education and Development.

SELECTED FACULTY

Robin Broad: Political economy of international development, with a particular focus on environment and development.
Fantu Cheru: Development in the African context.
David Hirschmann: Rural development, development management, decentralization, women and development.

Clark University

Graduate Programs in International Development, Community
Planning, and Environment
950 Main Street
Worcester, MA 01610-1477
Phone: 508-793-7201
Fax: 508-793-8820
Email: *idce@clarku.edu*
Web site: *www2.clarku.edu/newsite/departments/idce*
Degrees: B.A., M.A.

Clark University's Graduate Programs in International Development,
Community Planning, and Environment (IDCE) offers four master's
programs: International Development and Social Change (ID),
Community Planning (ID/CP), Geographic Information Sciences
for Development and Environment (GIS/DE), and Environmental
Sciences and Policy (ES&P). The IDCE master's degree requires ten
graduate courses and a research paper of publishable quality. The
minimum time necessary to complete these requirements is eighteen
months, but students often take two years. Many take additional
time for an internship, overseas research project, or applied training.
The IDCE graduate programs are recognized worldwide for action
research in resource management, gender and development,
geographic information systems, rural socioeconomic change, environmental risk analysis, and participatory community planning.

Undergraduates majoring in international development must
take orientation, specialization, and skills courses as well as fulfill
an internship requirement. Clark offers a five-year combined
B.A./M.A. in the field, and qualifying students may get tuition for
their fifth year waived.

COURSE HIGHLIGHTS: Child Labor and the State: Comparative
Perspectives/Urban Ecology: Cities as Ecosystems/Social Forestry,
Agroecology, and Development/Non-Governmental Organizations:
Catalysts for Development/Population, Environment, and
Development/Seminar in Resource Geography.

SELECTED FACULTY

William Fisher: Social and environmental impact of large dams, forced displacement, transnational advocacy, competition over natural resources, nongovernmental organizations.

Barbara Thomas-Slayter: Local institution-building; women and public policy; household and community resource management; dynamics of class, ethnicity, and gender in African development.

University of California, Berkeley

Office of Development Studies
101 Stephens Hall
Berkeley, CA 94720
Phone: 510-642-4466
Fax: 510-642-9850
Email: *iastp@uclink.berkeley.edu*
Web site: *www.ias.berkeley.edu/iastp/ds/ds10.html*
Degree: B.A.

The University of California at Berkeley offers an undergraduate major in Development Studies (DS). DS majors are required to take core courses in development theory and build upon this core with coursework focusing on a discipline, a geographic area, and methodological skills appropriate to the student's primary disciplinary interest. Proficiency in a foreign language is required, and a senior thesis option is available.

COURSE HIGHLIGHTS: US Agricultural Development in the 20th Century/Islands and Oceans/Public Policy and Administration in Developing Countries/Rhetoric of Imperialism/International Food and Nutrition Policies/Revolutionary Movements.

SELECTED FACULTY

Miguel Altieri: Agricultural ecology, sustainable agriculture development, alternative technologies in agriculture.

Pranab K. Bardhan: International trade, development economics.
David Collier: Latin American government and politics.
Ruth Collier: Comparative and historical study of labor in Latin America.
Alain de Janvry: International rural development.
Robert Reed: Urbanism and urbanization in the Third World, cultural and historical geography.

University of California, Davis
Community and Regional Development Program
Department of Human and Community Development
One Shields Avenue
Davis, CA 95616
Phone: 530-752-3558
Fax: 530-752-5660
Web site: *hcd.ucdavis.edu*
Degrees: B.S., M.S.

The Community and Regional Development (CRD) program at the University of California, Davis examines community and organizational development, the role of culture and ethnicity in shaping community life, and the ways in which knowledge can be used to solve social problems. Undergraduates opting for the Bachelor of Science degree choose from among four areas of specialization: community groups, organization and management, policy and planning, and social services. Completion of an internship is required. The Graduate Group in Community Development offers a multidisciplinary program of study leading to the Master of Science degree. Master's students may specialize in urban and rural development, community economic and political development, community design and planning, racial and ethnic relations, international migration and development, gender and community development, and social policy analysis.

Either program is recommended for students seeking careers in nonprofit administration, city and regional planning, organizational consulting, program evaluation, or social research.

COURSE HIGHLIGHTS: Community Development Theory/Transformation of Work/Political Economy of Transnational Migration/Ethnographic Research in America/Theory and Practice of Geography/Research Design and Method in Community Studies.

SELECTED FACULTY
Luis Guarnizo: Economic sociology, transnational migration, immigrant entrepreneurs, comparative international development, citizenship.
Martin Kenney: Technology and regional development, Japanese foreign direct investment and labor relations, maquiladoras, biotechnology and society.
Janet Momsen: Gender and development, tourism, gender and land rights, small-scale agriculture, regional geography of the Caribbean, Brazil, Central America, and China.
Miriam Wells: Political and economic anthropology, ethnicity, political brokerage, farm labor and US-Mexican migration, the social organization of agriculture.

School of Development Studies
University of East Anglia
Norwich NR4 7TJ
UNITED KINGDOM
Phone: +44 01603 592807
Fax: +44 01603 451999
Email: *dev.general@uea.ac.uk*
Web site: *www.uea.ac.uk/dev*
Degrees: B.A., B.Sc., M.A., M.Sc., M.Res., M.Phil., Ph.D.

The School of Development Studies (DEV) is one of the UK's premier development studies teaching and research institutions. The professional skills, experience, and interests of the School's thirty faculty cover both the social and natural sciences, from economics, sociology, gender, and politics, to environment, fisheries, soil science, and agronomy. DEV offers undergraduate, graduate, diploma, and research-based programs.

The faculty of DEV are also members of the Overseas Development Group (ODG) which was founded in 1967 and is a charitable company wholly owned by the University of East Anglia. The ODG is known worldwide for providing high quality research, training, and consultant services for international development. Since its foundation the ODG has completed over 700 assignments in more than seventy countries, and its clients include NGOs, governments, and national and international development agencies. The ODG provides DEV staff with opportunities to participate in ongoing development work; this real world experience adds a valuable element to the School's teaching programs.

The Dean of Students' office at the university distributes an International Student Handbook, available online at *www.uea.ac.uk/dos/international.html*.

COURSE HIGHLIGHTS: Development Studies Epistemologies/ Industrialization and Industrial Policy/Research Skills for Social Analysis/Education Policies and Practice for Development/ Macroeconomic and Trade Policy/Rural Policies.

SELECTED FACULTY

Jonathan Barton: Comparative environmental policy, industry and environment, urban environmental management, political economy of the regulatory state.

Rajat Ganguly: International security, world politics, conflict resolution, peace studies, nationalism, ethnic politics, human rights, political development.

Richard Palmer Jones: Poverty, work and households, natural resources and the environment, agricultural production, irrigation and water resource development.

Jennifer Leith: Rural development and rural development planning, social assessment, local culture and livelihood issues concerning natural resources, gender.

University of Sussex
Institute of Development Studies
Brighton BN1 9RE
UNITED KINGDOM
Phone: +44 0 1273 606261
Fax: +44 0 1273 621202/691647
Email: *ids@ids.ac.uk*
Web site: *www.ids.ac.uk/ids/teach*
Degrees: M.A., M.Phil., D.Phil.

The Institute of Development Studies (IDS) at Sussex University runs the Development Studies Graduate Research Center (GRC). Established in 1966 as an independent research institute, IDS is the longest-established and largest center in Europe for interdisciplinary graduate studies in development issues. From its earliest years of teaching and training with an emphasis on interdisciplinary study, the institute has played a central and continuing part in international debates on development theory and policy.

IDS and the Development Studies GRC offer a two-year course-work Master of Philosophy (M.Phil.) in development studies, a one-year M.A. in gender and development (run jointly with the Culture, Development, and the Environment GRC), a one-year M.A. in governance and development, and the supervision of students working for the degree of Doctor of Philosophy (D.Phil.).

The International and Study Abroad Office *(www.sussex.ac.uk/ international/sussex)* provides information of use to overseas students.

COURSE HIGHLIGHTS: Competing in the Global Economy/ Issues in Environment and Development/Public Sector Management/Rules of Engagement in International Trade and Finance/Social Sectors in Development Policy/Agriculture and Rural Development.

SELECTED FACULTY

Stephen Devereux: Food security, coping strategies, and poverty reduction with particular reference to Africa, especially Ghana and Namibia.

John Gaventa: Citizen participation, power, participatory research and education methodologies, participatory governance.

Khalid Nadvi: Industrial development, industrial organization, employment generation and technical change with a particular focus on small and medium enterprises.

Howard White: Aid policy issues (especially the macroeconomic and poverty impact of aid), macroeconomic policy and modeling, determinants of social indicators.

University of Wisconsin, Madison

Ph.D. in Development Studies Program
Land Tenure Center
1357 University Avenue
Madison, WI 53715
Phone: 608-262-3412
Fax: 608-262-2141
Email: *devstudies-ltc@facstaff.wisc.edu*
Web site: *www.wisc.edu/ltc*
Degree: Ph.D.

The University of Wisconsin's doctoral program in development studies, based in the College of Agricultural and Life Sciences, trains social and technical scientists for careers in development assistance agencies, voluntary organizations, or foundations working in developing countries. The program is both problem and theory oriented, and draws on the expertise of faculty concerned with international issues in many different departments. Students seeking admission must already hold a master's degree, preferably in one of the disciplines relevant to development. Previous experience living and working in a Third World country is an important aspect of a successful applicant's background. Each applicant must submit a research proposal, which will form the cornerstone of the student's work. Overseeing the program is the Land Tenure Center, which provides research, training, and technical assistance throughout the world on issues of land tenure and land use, agrarian reform, land markets, legislative drafting, land registration and titling, institutional dimensions of rural development, and environmental/natural resource management.

COURSE HIGHLIGHTS: Energy, Environment, and Development/ Macroeconomics of Agricultural Development/Sociology of Economic Change/Development Policy Analysis/Seminar in Rural Community Economics.

SELECTED FACULTY

Michael R. Carter: Problems of agrarian transformations and class transitions.
Jess C. Gilbert: Historical and comparative approach to the study of agriculture, family farming, and rural land ownership.
Harvey M. Jacobs: Public policy for land use and environmental management, global spread of private property as a social institution, conservative challenges to mainstream land use and environmental movements in the US.
Florencia Mallon: Social movements, agrarian history, political culture, nationalism, indigenous history, 19th- and 20th-century Latin America.

ECONOMICS

American University
Department of Economics
4400 Massachusetts Avenue NW

Washington, DC 20016-8029
Phone: 202-885-3770
Fax: 202-885-3790
Email: *econ@american.edu*
Web site: *www.american.edu/academic.depts/cas/econ/econ.html*
Degrees: B.A., M.A., Ph.D.

The Economics Department at American University offers two majors in economics and economic theory. Within each major, students may choose a general or international track. The economic theory major provides rigorous training in economic theory, econometrics, and quantitative skills and prepares the student for a research position or graduate work in economics. The economics major combines economic theory with applied fields and is designed to allow the student the flexibility of a double major with other departments at the university.

The department offers three master's programs. The M.A. program in economics provides training in diverse theoretical approaches and empirical methods and experience in applications to current economic problems. The M.A. in financial economics for public policy is designed for the student or professional interested in developing theoretical and practical skills in economic analysis and financial markets. The M.A. in development finance and banking focuses on financial markets, project financing, and banking and provides analytical depth in macro-, development, and international economics. The department's Ph.D. program has two tracks: the mainstream economics track and the more heterodox political economy track.

The Globalization in Crisis program sponsors conferences, seminars, and workshops to address issues related to economic globalization.

COURSE HIGHLIGHTS: The Global Majority/Social Choice and Economic Justice/Economics of Antitrust and Regulation/Energy Economics, Resources, and the Environment/Seminar in Labor Economics/Economics of the World Regions.

SELECTED FACULTY

Robin Hahnel: Participatory economics, effects of globalization.
Mieke Meurs: Comparative economic systems and development with special attention to Eastern Europe.
John Willoughby: Political economy of globalization in the Middle East and South Asia, Marxist and institutional political economy, modern economic history.
Jon Wisman: Methodology, history of economic thought, general economic history, workplace democracy.

University of California, Riverside

Department of Economics
1150 University Avenue
Riverside, CA 92521-0427
Phone: 909-787-5037
Fax: 909-787-5685
Web site: *www.economics.ucr.edu*
Degrees: B.A., M.A., Ph.D.

The University of California, Riverside offers B.A. degrees in economics, business economics, economics/administrative studies, and economics/law and society.

The graduate program in economics prepares students for research and teaching in academic institutions as well as for positions in government, international agencies, and the private sector. The one-year M.A. degree is designed as a preparatory program for those students interested in pursuing the Ph.D. who are not adequately prepared to enter the doctoral program directly (e.g., those who lack prerequisites in economics or mathematics, or who have been out of school for some time). Doctoral students first complete a core curriculum in economic theory and quantitative methods. The department encourages applicants from a variety of backgrounds, but a good understanding of intermediate micro- and macroeconomics, multivariate calculus, and elementary linear algebra is necessary to begin taking the core courses.

COURSE HIGHLIGHTS: Political Economy of Imperialism/ Project Evaluation in Developing Countries/Labor Institutions and Macro Labor Outcomes/Women's Labor and the Economy/ Trade, Globalization, and Development/Natural Resource Economics.

SELECTED FACULTY

Susan B. Carter: Historical perspectives on the labor market, household behavior, education, discrimination, population dynamics.
Stephen Cullenberg: Economic methodology, international political economy, Marxian economics.
Gary Dymski: Money and banking, political economy, urban economics, macroeconomics.
Steven Helfand: Development economics, agricultural economics, Brazil, Latin America, the political economy of agricultural policy in Brazil.

University of Massachusetts, Amherst

Department of Economics
Thompson Hall
Amherst, MA 01003
Phone (undergraduate): 413-545-0855
Phone (graduate): 413-545-2082
Fax: 413-545-2921
Email: *econs@econs.umass.edu*
Web site: *www.umass.edu/economics*
Degrees: B.A., M.A., Ph.D.

The Department of Economics at the University of Massachusetts, Amherst offers the B.A., M.A., and Ph.D. All economics majors take courses in two basic areas: micro- and macroeconomics, and statistics and mathematics. Students choose the remaining courses themselves, in accordance with their interests and career objectives. Every student has the option of substituting a five-course collateral field composed of courses taken outside of economics for two required economics courses; examples of such fields are history, international relations, business management, and political science. All members of the faculty teach undergraduate courses and are accessible to undergraduate students. Of related interest is the major in social thought and political economy, which draws on resources from a variety of disciplines, economics among them.

The graduate program is designed primarily for doctoral candidates, but a Master of Arts in economics is awarded along the way. Course requirements for the master's are the same as for the Ph.D., and a thesis is optional. Students must complete one semester each of macroeconomics, political economy, and mathematical methods for economists (if necessary), and two semesters each of microeconomics, econometrics, and introduction to economic history. Students are required to complete two courses in each of two advanced theory or applied fields of economics and pass two comprehensive exams before embarking on the dissertation.

The department is home to the Association for Economic and Social Analysis and the Political Economy Research Institute.

COURSE HIGHLIGHTS: Advanced Marxian Economics/Social Control of Business/Labor Markets and Employment/Political Economy of Capitalism/Latin American Economic Development/ Capitalism, Socialism, and Democracy: Three Utopias and Their Critics.

SELECTED FACULTY

Samuel Bowles: Co-evolution of preferences, institutions, and behavior; economic and other consequences of inequality in modern economies.

Carmen D. Deere: Women and development, peasant household economics, agrarian reform, organization of production in the transition to socialism.

Gerald Epstein: Determinants of central bank policy in open economies, political economy of international credit relations, political economy of capital controls.

Robert Pollin: Financial macroeconomics, political economy, living wage proposals.

Richard Wolff: Marxian economics, class aspects of the problems of contemporary capitalism, systematic comparisons of alternative economic theories.

New School University
Department of Economics, Room 350
Graduate Faculty of Political and Social Science
65 Fifth Avenue
New York, NY 10003
Phone: 212-229-5717
Fax: 212-229-5724
Email: *gfadmit@newschool.edu*
Web site: *www.newschool.edu/gf/econ*
Degrees: M.A., Ph.D., D.S.Sc.

The Department of Economics at New School University is committed to a broad, critical, and historical approach to the study of economics and the application of modern analytical tools to the study of real economic problems. It offers a supportive community within which students can pursue innovative research and study in fields of political economy, money and finance, international and development economics, economic policy, the history of economic thought, and economic theory. At the master's level, students may concentrate in economics, economics and finance, and classical or interdisciplinary political economy. Degree requirements consist of three core courses, five concentration courses, two electives, and a written examination. A recently instituted M.A. in global political economy and finance consists of a required curriculum of six courses (covering topics in economic theory, econometrics, finance, and the historical foundations and current problems of political economy); a required internship or mentored research; and three elective courses at the M.A. or higher level.

Students in the M.A. program are not automatically accepted for study toward the Ph.D. degree; separate admission to the Ph.D. program must be obtained. At the doctoral level, required core courses in Marxian, post-Keynesian, and neo-Ricardian theory supplement core courses in microeconomics, macroeconomics, and econometrics. Candidates fulfill requirements in both foreign language and mathematics and complete written and oral examinations before beginning the dissertation.

The Center for Economic Policy Analysis (CEPA) is the research center for New School's Economics Department. Faculty members employ graduate students from the department as assistants on research projects. The three main areas of particular emphasis at CEPA are macroeconomic policy, inequality and poverty, and globalization.

COURSE HIGHLIGHTS: Economics of Race, Class, and Gender/ Seminar in Labor and Political Economy/Transformational Growth/Emergence of Capitalism/Political Economy of the Environment/Money, Credit, and Economic Activity.

SELECTED FACULTY

Duncan Foley: Complex evolutionary dynamics; foundations of statistical inference; technical change and global warming; long-run patterns of population growth, wealth, and income distribution; economic development.

William Milberg: Labor market effects of foreign trade and investment, philosophy of post-war American economic thought.

Anwar Shaikh: Political economy, macroeconomic growth and cycles, international trade, credit and inflation, US stock market, international comparisons of the welfare state.

Lance Taylor: Macroeconomic stabilization and adjustment in developing and transition economies, capital markets, reconstruction of macroeconomic theory.

University of Notre Dame
Department of Economics
245 O'Shaughnessy Hall
Notre Dame, IN 46556
Phone: 219-631-5479
Fax: 219-631-8809
Email: *skurski.1@nd.edu*
Web site: *www.nd.edu/~economic*
Degrees: B.A., M.A., Ph.D.

The graduate program in economics at the University of Notre Dame distinguishes itself by receptivity to alternative theoretical approaches and methodologies and a commitment to research related to issues of economic and social justice. The curriculum provides a systematic grounding in the major paradigms of economic analysis; ideas from the neoclassical, post-Keynesian, neo-Marxian, and institutional traditions are critically examined. Students pursue independent research using mathematical and econometric procedures, case studies, and other forms of institutional analysis.

Graduate students specialize in one of three field clusters: development and international economics; economic theory, the history of economic thought and methodology; and institutions (such as labor, financial, industrial, and public institutions). Individually tailored clusters are also permitted. The department offers both a research (thesis required) and a non-research master's degree. The doctoral program encourages completion of the degree in four years. Under normal circumstances, students will complete their coursework within two years, write their comprehensive examinations at the end of their first year, and in the third year develop, present, and defend their dissertation proposal. Writing and defending the dissertation completes the doctoral program.

Undergraduates majoring in economics must take three core courses, three distribution courses, and two electives, as well as fulfill a writing requirement.

COURSE HIGHLIGHTS: Problems in Political Economy/Growth and Distribution Theory/Labor Institutions/Open Economy Macroeconomics/Approaches to Inner City Economic Development/Appropriate Technology and Third World Development.

SELECTED FACULTY

Charles Craypo: Labor economics, effects of corporate consolidation and union decline.

Amitava Dutt: Growth and distribution theory, post-Keynesian macroeconomic theory, development and international economics.

Denis Goulet: Comparative development strategies, environmental and economic ethics, interdisciplinary research methods, culture and development.

David Ruccio: Methodology, development, international political economy, Latin America, planning.

University of Utah
Department of Economics
1645 East Central Campus Drive
Room 308
Salt Lake City, UT 84112-9300
Phone: 801-581-7481
Fax: 801-585-5649
Email (undergraduate): *mayne@economics.utah.edu*
Email (graduate): *gollaher@economics.utah.edu*
Web site: *web.econ.utah.edu*
Degrees: B.A., B.S., M.A., M.S., M.Phil., Ph.D.

Students majoring in economics at the University of Utah take five core courses: two from among the area groupings of econometrics, economic thought, and economic history; four electives; and several allied credit courses in related but separate departments.

The M.S. or M.A. degree prepares economists for work in a variety of contexts, either in the public or private sectors. Two tracks are offered: the general program, which provides broad training in economics and requires a minimum of thirty semester hours of coursework; and the applied program, which is oriented toward technical and analytical training and requires strong mathematical and statistical background. Research internships are encouraged for the latter program, which awards a certificate in applied research along with the M.A. The Ph.D. program prepares students for professional careers in teaching, research, business, and government; it provides broad mastery of both theoretical and applied fields and both orthodox and heterodox approaches. The department attempts to provide students receiving financial aid with teaching opportunities.

COURSE HIGHLIGHTS: Industrialization and Economic Development: The American Case/Capitalism and Socialism/ Discrimination in the Labor Market/Poverty and Inequality/ Markets and Government: The Economics of Cooperation/ Environmental and Natural Resource Economics.

SELECTED FACULTY

Al Campbell: Economics of socialism, economic planning, economics of co-ops, the Cuban economy, industrial organization, dynamic macroeconomic models.
Hans Ehrbar: Labor theory of value, critical realism, historical materialism, Marxian theories of money and credit, theory of capitalist democracy, economic planning.
Kenneth Jameson: Financial systems in Latin America and Eastern Europe, history of development thinking.
Peter Philips: Labor market analysis; unions and collective bargaining; racial, ethnic, age, and gender differences in the labor market; immigration; child labor issues.

EDUCATION

University of California, Los Angeles
Department of Education
Graduate School of Education and Information Studies
Moore Hall 2320C, Box 951521
Los Angeles, CA 90095-1521
Phone: 310-825-2624
Email: *info@gseis.ucla.edu*
Web site: *www.gseis.ucla.edu/ded.html*
Degrees: M.A., M.Ed., Ph.D., Ed.D.

UCLA's Graduate School of Education and Information Studies (GSEIS) supports many graduate programs in education. The Urban Schooling: Curriculum, Teaching, Leadership, and Policy Studies Division offers programs of doctoral study leading to the Ph.D. degree, with emphases in administrative studies, education policy analysis, and curriculum theory and teaching studies. The division of Social Sciences and Comparative Education offers Ph.D. and M.A. degree programs in four areas of specialization: philosophical/historical studies in education; cultural studies in education, race and ethnic studies in education, and comparative/international studies in education.

Center X, a research and outreach center affiliated with GSEIS, sponsors numerous collaborative projects with communities and school systems in the Los Angeles area. Its Teacher Education Program grants a teaching credential with a social justice emphasis. At the undergraduate level, the Department of Education offers a minor in education studies.

COURSE HIGHLIGHTS: Education and National Development/ Nonformal Education in Cross-Cultural Perspective/Student Problems: Social Context/Problems and Issues in Bilingual and

Multicultural Education/Special Topics in Urban Schooling/ Social Contexts of Literacy Learning.

SELECTED FACULTY

Douglas Kellner: Critical theory and education, cultural studies, media studies.

Peter McLaren: Post-colonial, postmodern, and Marxist theories applied to curriculum development and instruction; critical multiculturalism, ethnography, and literacy.

Edith Mukudi: Gender; access, participation, and funding of education; nutrition and education participation linkages; policy and practice; African education.

Robert Rhoads: Organizational analysis, democratic movements in higher education, Latin American higher education, and qualitative/ethnographic methods.

Daniel Solorzano: Sociology of education; social mobility; critical race and gender theory; marginality; racial, ethnic, gender, and class relations with a special emphasis on the educational access, persistence, and graduation of US minority students.

Ontario Institute for Studies in Education
University of Toronto
252 Bloor Street West
Toronto, Ontario
CANADA M5S 1V6
Phone: 416-923-6641
Fax: 416-926-4725
Email: *gradstudy@oise.utoronto.ca*
Web site: *www.oise.utoronto.ca*
Degrees: M.A., M.Ed., Ph.D., Ed.D.

The University of Toronto's Ontario Institute for Studies in Education (OISE) consists of five departments: Adult Education, Community Development, and Counseling Psychology; Curriculum, Teaching, and Learning; Human Development and

Applied Psychology; Sociology and Equity Studies in Education; and Theory and Policy Studies in Education. Several graduate degrees are available, including an interdepartmental master's and doctoral program in comparative, international, and development education. Research foci at the graduate level include critical pedagogy and cultural studies, global education, learning and work, aboriginal and indigenous studies, and nature and development of literacy. OISE is home to many research centers and scholarly publications, among them *trans/forms: insurgent voices in education*, a graduate student journal.

The University's International Student Center *(www.library. utoronto.ca/isc/index.htm)* supplies information on visas, immigration, financial aid, and other relevant matters to students from outside Canada.

COURSE HIGHLIGHTS: Racism, Law, and Radical Education/ Eco-Sociology/Innovations in Education: A Comparative Analysis/Curriculum, Popular Culture, and Social Difference/ Critical Ethnography/Modernization, Development, and Education in African Contexts.

SELECTED FACULTY

Budd Hall: Adult education and global civil society, participatory research, critical environmental adult education, comparative and international studies in adult education.
Edmund V. O'Sullivan: Global ecological education, critical pedagogy, holistic education, community development.
Ruth Roach Pierson: Race, class, and gender in historical sociology; women and colonialism, imperialism, and nationalism; feminist studies in education.
Daniel Schugurensky: Popular education, citizenship learning, participatory democracy, Latin America, political sociology of adult education, university-community relationships.

University of St. Thomas
Curriculum and Instruction
School of Education
1000 LaSalle Avenue
Minneapolis, MN 55403
Phone: 651-962-4460
Email: *soe_candi@stthomas.edu*
Web site: *www.stthomas.edu/education/*
Degree: Ph.D.

The University of St. Thomas recently instituted a doctoral program in critical pedagogy. Contact the School of Education for more details.

University of San Francisco
School of Education
2350 Turk Boulevard
San Francisco, CA 94117
Phone: 415-422-6525
Email: *kohl@usfca.edu*
Web site: *www.soe.usfca.edu/*
Degree: M.A.

The University of San Francisco's Center for Teaching Excellence and Social Justice grants a Master of Arts in teaching; graduates are eligible to secure further credentials in California. The program focuses on school reform in urban settings.

ENVIRONMENTAL STUDIES

University of California, Santa Cruz
Environmental Studies Department

339 Natural Sciences 2
Santa Cruz, CA 95064
Phone: 831-459-2634
Fax: 831-459-4015
Email: *studies@zzyx.ucsc.edu*
Web site: *zzyx.ucsc.edu/ES/es.html*
Degrees: B.A., Ph.D.

The Environmental Studies Department at the University of California, Santa Cruz focuses on the sustainability of human and ecological systems. Students pursue an interdisciplinary curriculum that combines coursework in ecology and the social sciences. Special emphasis is placed on the topics of sustainable agriculture, conservation of biodiversity and natural ecosystems, and the design of policies and institutions that reconcile environmental and social priorities. As a complement to classroom instruction and research, the Environmental Studies Field and Internship program places approximately two hundred students each year with government agencies, community organizations, and private firms. Students are encouraged to participate in faculty-directed research on specific problems.

The Ph.D. program in environmental studies provides advanced training for students committed to addressing complex social and ecological problems from an interdisciplinary viewpoint. Close faculty-student interaction, department-wide intellectual exchange, and flexibility for continued innovation are emphasized. The interdisciplinary nature of the core curriculum requires rigorous preparation at the undergraduate level. Students seeking admission to the doctoral program should have an advanced basic knowledge of ecology and genetics, macro- and microeconomics, politics, and political economy, either from prior coursework or advanced independent reading. Prospective students should contact faculty directly to inquire about specific course requirements and sponsorship.

COURSE HIGHLIGHTS: Sustainable Development and Environmental Issues at the US-Mexico Border/Field Ethnobotany/Political Ecology and Social Change/Social Theories of Nature/Restoration Ecology/Public Policy and Conservation/Sustainable Agriculture, Food Politics, and Community Networks.

SELECTED FACULTY

Stephen Gliessman: Agroecology, sustainable agriculture, tropical land use and development, ecology and management of California vegetation.
David Goodman: Political economy of international environmental issues, global agri-food systems, North-South relations and sustainable development.
Daniel Press: US environmental politics and policy, social capital and democratic theory, industrial ecology, land and species conservation, regionalism.
S. Ravi Rajan: Large technological systems and risk, urban environmental politics, North-South environmental conflicts, environmental social theory, environmental ethics.
Carol Shennan: Ecosystem studies, agriculture-wetland interactions, participatory research, gender and environmental issues.

Dickinson College
Department of Environmental Studies
PO Box 1773
Carlisle, PA 17013
Phone: 717-245-1355
Fax: 717-245-1971
Web site: *www.dickinson.edu/departments/envst*
Degrees: B.S., B.A.

One of the oldest and strongest programs of its kind in the nation, Dickinson's Environmental Studies Department offers two independent majors, a B.S. in environmental science and a B.A. in environmental studies. In addition to providing a sound academic background for students, the college actively promotes community outreach and training. Students and faculty are involved at the local, regional, and national levels working cooperatively with grassroots activists, government agencies, and the private sector on a wide variety of environmental problems, ranging from monitoring acid rain and storm water runoff to helping communities track toxic emissions from nearby factories. Several overseas field research programs are available as well.

Courses give students a background in the natural processes working at the surface of the earth to provide a basis for evaluation and control of environmental quality; the philosophical and historical foundations for the human relationship with those processes; and the economic, social, and political contexts for environmental decision-making. All courses are interdisciplinary in nature, content, and approach, and attempt to provide models for future alternatives. All students take a core curriculum, which includes courses from environmental science, environmental ethics, environmental economics, environmental policy, and a senior seminar. Students may then choose a track in either natural science or humanities and social science, designing a cluster of courses focused around a theme of their choice to fulfill the remaining course requirements.

COURSE HIGHLIGHTS: Environmental Disruption and Policy Analysis/Ecological Anthropology/Modeling Environmental Interactions/International Environmental Challenges/ Environmental Economics/Analysis and Management of the Aquatic Environment.

SELECTED FACULTY

Michael Heiman: Environmental regulation and planning; solid, hazardous, and nuclear waste management; sustainable development; environmental racism and justice.
Brian S. Pedersen: Effects of environmental stresses on trees and forests, environmental problems of post-communist countries.

Candie Wilderman: Watershed assessment for land use planning, biological monitoring of streams, urban storm water runoff assessment, grassroots environmental activism.

Evergreen State College
Graduate Program in Environmental Studies
Olympia, WA 98505
Phone: 360-867-6707
Email: *mes@evergreen.edu*
Web site: *www.evergreen.edu/user/grad/mes/home.htm*
Degree: M.E.S.

The Evergreen State College's Graduate Program in Environmental Studies, initiated in 1984, integrates the study of environmental science and public policy and leads to the Master of Environmental Studies (MES) degree. The program's goal is to provide quality professional preparation for people working at the interface between environmental science and policymaking in the public, private, and nonprofit sectors. The perspectives of the MES Program are national and international, but extensive use is made of the environmental issues of the Pacific Northwest.

All MES students take four programs in sequence to complete the core curriculum: political, economic, and ecological processes; population, energy, and resources; case studies: environmental assessment, policy, and management; and quantitative analysis and research methods for environmental studies. Elective courses and a thesis are also required. Students are recommended for candidacy or full admission upon satisfactory completion of all requirements of the first two core programs. Working students may pursue the degree on a part-time basis; electives and thesis work are available during the summer.

COURSE HIGHLIGHTS: Conserving and Restoring Biodiversity/ Wetland Ecology and Management/Salmonid Ecology/ Pesticides/Natural Resource Economics/Geographic Information Systems Analysis/Tribal Natural Resource Policy/Forest Ecology.

SELECTED FACULTY

Peter Bohmer: Neoliberalism and its alternatives, political economy of racism, wealth and income inequality in the US.
Russell Fox: Community development; affordable housing; agricultural preservation; community land trusts, economics, and currencies; participatory research.
Nalini Nadkarni: Silviculture and forest ecology.
Zahid Shariff: Government budgeting and fiscal policy, public bureaucracies, comparative politics and administration.

Humboldt State University
Environment and Community Graduate Program
John M. Meyer, Graduate Coordinator
Department of Government and Politics
Arcata, CA 95521
Phone: 707-826-4497
Fax: 707-826-4496
Email: *jmm7001@humboldt.edu*
Web site: *www.humboldt.edu/~mass*
Degree: M.A.

The mission of the Environment and Community program at Humboldt State University is to prepare students to understand the relationship between communities and their environment, to analyze environmental and community issues, and to act effectively in situations where values and interests diverge. The Master of Arts is a two-year, full-time cohort program, or one in which a group of enrollees all begin and complete coursework at the same time. Six seminars, three elective courses, and participation in a colloquium are required of all students. During the last semester of the program, students will either write a master's thesis or complete a full-time internship and develop a related project.

COURSE HIGHLIGHTS: Rights, Politics, and the Environment/ Environment and Ecosystem Analysis/Resource Planning in Rural Communities/Politics of Appropriate Technology in the Third World/North American Environmental History/ Economics of Antitrust and Regulation.

SELECTED FACULTY

Susan Armstrong: Environmental ethics.
Sing Chew: Environmental sociology, world development, globalization, bioregionalism, deep ecology.
Yvonne Everett: Applied forest and landscape ecology, management of nontimber forest products, community forestry, land use planning and management.
John M. Meyer: Environmental politics and political theory; the relationship of environmentalist concerns to conceptions of politics, property, and rights.

University of Michigan

School of Natural Resources and Environment
Dana Building
430 East University
Ann Arbor, MI 48109-1115
Phone: 734-764-6453
Fax: 734-615-1277
Email (graduate): *snre.gradteam@umich.edu*
Email (undergraduate): *snre.undergradteam@umich.edu*
Web site: *www.snre.umich.edu*
Degrees: B.S., M.S., Ph.D.

The School of Natural Resources and Environment (SNRE) at the University of Michigan is dedicated to protecting the earth's resources and achieving a sustainable society. SNRE's faculty and students strive to generate knowledge, develop innovative policies, and refine new techniques. Through research and teaching, the program prepares practitioners to manage and conserve natural and environmental resources to meet the full range of human needs on a sustainable basis. SNRE maintains a relatively small enrollment of 400 undergraduate students, to provide the personal attention, sense of community, contact with faculty, counseling support, and friendly atmosphere of a small school. An honors program, research collaborations with faculty, and field study opportunities are all available to undergraduates.

The School of Natural Resources and Environment offers a Master of Science in natural resources; interested students may apply to one of two plans: resource policy and behavior or resource ecology and management. Students in both sections take core, distribution, analytic, and cognate courses and write a master's thesis. Requirements for the degree generally take two years to complete. SNRE's doctoral program in natural resources and environment trains exceptional students for original research and scholarship at the forefront of their chosen fields. The program is highly individualized; each student prepares a detailed course of study in cooperation with his/her advisor and other relevant faculty.

Environmental justice is a highly regarded specialization offered at the undergraduate, master's, and doctoral levels.

COURSE HIGHLIGHTS: Social Change, Energy, and Land Ethics/ Social Impact Assessment/Environmental Justice: Domestic and International/Human Resource Ecology/Agroforestry/ Negotiation Skills in Environmental Dispute Resolution.

SELECTED FACULTY

Steven Brechin: Sociology of international organizations, transnational social movements, social barriers to environmental policy and technical interventions, population-environment dynamics in the developing world.
Bunyan Bryant: Small group organization, advocacy, social change, impact of differential exposures of contaminants on people of color and low-income communities.
Gloria Helfand: Regulating non-point source pollution, economics of pollution prevention, economics of natural resources management, timber economics.

Ivette Perfecto: Agroforestry and ecosystems management with emphasis on tropical agroecosystems and forests, biological control, sustainable development in Latin America.

University of Oregon
Environmental Studies Program
10 Pacific Hall
Eugene, OR 97403-5223
Phone: 541-346-5000
Fax: 541-346-5954
Email: *ecostudy@oregon.uoregon.edu*
Web site: *darkwing.uoregon.edu/~ecostudy/*
Degrees: B.A., B.S., M.A., M.S., Ph.D.

Students at the University of Oregon's Environmental Studies program have the opportunity to integrate coursework in the sciences, social sciences, and humanities, as well as the professional programs of management, public policy, design, and law. The program offers undergraduate and graduate training leading to a B.A. or B.S. in environmental studies or environmental science, an M.A. or M.S. in environmental studies, or a Ph.D. in environmental science, studies, and policy (ESSP). The Environmental Studies program offers courses at both introductory and advanced levels; however, the bulk of degree requirements will be fulfilled through an approved list of courses offered by other departments around campus.

At the undergraduate level, students may pursue internships, self-initiated projects, or an honors option. The M.S. or M.A. degree can be completed in two years, but generally takes candidates about two-and-a-half years. The university offers a flexible, explicitly interdisciplinary, largely student-designed master's program, without extensive lists of required courses or tracks. The ESSP doctorate, initiated in 1997, provides solid professional preparation for academic and research occupations as well as for leadership roles in creating and implementing environmental solutions in the business sector.

COURSE HIGHLIGHTS: Environmental Justice/Watershed Planning/Public Lands/Sociology of Developing Areas/Resource and Environmental Economics/Biological Diversity/Solar and Renewable Energies/Seminar in Sustainable Tourism/Social Ecology.

SELECTED FACULTY

Robert Collin: Environmental justice, environmental and urban policy.
Galen Martin: Conservation and communities, environmental geography.
Peter Walker: Human–environment relations, Africa, political ecology, the American West.

ETHNIC STUDIES

University of California, Berkeley
Department of Ethnic Studies
506 Barrows Hall #2570
Berkeley, CA 94720-2570
Phone: 510-643-0796
Fax: 510-642-6456
Email: *ethnicst@socrates.berkeley.edu*
Web site: *socrates.berkeley.edu/~ethnicst/*
Degrees: B.A., Ph.D.

The Department of Ethnic Studies at the University of California, Berkeley comprises programs in Asian American, Native American, Chicano, and general ethnic studies. Each program grants a Bachelor of Arts degree requiring twelve courses. The Ethnic Studies Graduate Group offers a comparative ethnic studies Ph.D. focusing on the historical and sociocultural study of the core racial groups in United States history: Native Americans, African Americans, Asian Americans, and Chicanos and Latinos. Interdisciplinary in approach, it encourages students to adopt a broad range of theories and methods to analyze the construction of these racial ethno-cultural groups in relation to each other, in the Euro-American context, and in a transnational context. The doctoral program's courses are taught, and its students advised, by faculty not only from the Department of Ethnic Studies but also from other departments. Students may enter with either a B.A. or an M.A. degree. Proficiency in a language other than English is required.

COURSE HIGHLIGHTS: Politics, Public Policy, and Asian American Communities/Social Conflict in Latin America/ Africans in Indian Country/Series in Comparative Transnational Theories and Methods/The Southern Border/Law and Culture/ Racial Inequality in America.

SELECTED FACULTY

Evelyn Nakano Glenn: Women, work, and technology issues; labor histories of women of color; intersection of race, class, and gender.

Patricia Hilden: Early history of indigenous North America; representations of gender, ethnicity, and race in public venues, including museums and festivals.

Beatriz Manz: Ecological consequences of agricultural export production; indigenous, migrant, and refugee populations; political ecology; peasantry; US/Mexico border region.

Ling-chi Wang: Asian American history and civil rights issues, overseas Chinese, US foreign policies in Asia, bilingual education, Asian Americans in higher education.

University of California, Los Angeles
Center for African American Studies
Email: *admin@caas.ucla.edu*
Web site: *www.sscnet.ucla.edu/caas*
Degrees: B.A., M.A.

American Indian Studies Center
Email: *aisc@ucla.edu*
Web site: *www.sscnet.ucla.edu/indian*
Degree: M.A., J.D./M.A.

Asian American Studies Center
Email: *dtn@ucla.edu*
Web site: *www.sscnet.ucla.edu/aasc*
Degrees: B.A., M.A.

César E. Chávez Center for Chicana and Chicano Studies
Email: *chavez-info@csrc.ucla.edu*
Web site: *www.sscnet.ucla.edu/chavez*
Degree: B.A.

The University of California, Los Angeles boasts four centers administering separate interdisciplinary programs in ethnic studies. The Center for African American Studies supports research, publication, and outreach programs and offers the bachelor's and master's degrees. Students are expected to select a disciplinary concentration from among participating departments; at the master's level, these are anthropology, English, history, linguistics, music, philosophy, political science, psychology, and sociology. The American Indian Studies Center offers an M.A. and combination J.D./M.A.; the areas of concentration for the former are history and law, expressive arts, social relations and language, and literature and folklore. UCLA has one of the largest teaching programs in Asian American Studies in the nation, and has been one of two major sites for the training of Asian American studies scholars for the past twenty-five years. A Master of Arts and an undergraduate major are offered, and a Ph.D. in Asian American studies is under development. The B.A. in Chicana and Chicano studies is taught by a core faculty representing the fields of art, cultural studies, history, Latin American literature, sociolinguistics, and urban planning, and by an associated faculty from a variety of other disciplines.

COURSE HIGHLIGHTS: Growth Machines and Globalization/ Investigative Journalism and Communities of Color/Culture Change and the Mexican People/Critical Issues in US-Asia Relations/Nation Building: Developing Tribal Governments and Courts.

SELECTED FACULTY

Duane Champagne: Social and political change in American Indian communities.
Robert Hill: Marcus Garvey, C.L.R. James, Pan-Africanism, history of the Rastafari religion, Ethiopianism, history and ideology of Black popular culture.
Don Nakanishi: Educational politics and comparative minority politics, with special emphasis on the Asian American experience.
Abel Valenzuela: Minority groups in labor markets and impoverished communities, local economic impacts of immigration, issues related to welfare reform.

University of Colorado, Boulder
Department of Ethnic Studies
Ketchum 30, Campus Box 339
Boulder, CO 80309-0339
Phone: 303-492-8852
Fax: 303-492-7799
Email: *ethnic.studies@colorado.edu*
Web site: *www.colorado.edu/ethnicstudies*
Degree: B.A.

Created in 1996, the Department of Ethnic Studies at the University of Colorado maintains a full-time faculty of ten with several affiliated faculty in outside departments. In addition to the general requirements of the undergraduate college, majors must complete at least 33 semester hours of ethnic studies requirements which consist of 12 hours of required ethnic studies core courses, 12 hours in a primary ethnic-specific concentration, six hours in a secondary ethnic-specific concentration, and three hours in an ethnic studies course with a cross-cultural comparative focus. A comparative ethnic studies concentration option is also available upon consultation with and approval of the department chair.

While the Department of Ethnic Studies does not currently offer graduate degrees in the field, its faculty actively work to recruit African-American, American Indian, Chicano/Latino, and Asian/Pacific students for graduate studies at the university, with special attention given to students who are interested in carrying out theses and/or dissertations that involve substantive and theoretical work revolving around the broad topic of ethnicity and race in America. Faculty are further committed to the intellectual mentoring of such students, which might include instruction in graduate courses, administration of directed reading courses, service on students' M.A. or Ph.D. committees, or assistance with employment goals.

COURSE HIGHLIGHTS: Race, Class, and Pollution Politics/ Racist Ideology in American Life/Contemporary Black Protest Movements/Chicana Feminism and Knowledge/Indian-Government Conflicts: The FBI on Pine Ridge/Immigrant Women in the Global Economy.

SELECTED FACULTY
Evelyn Hu-DeHart: The Asian diaspora in Latin America and the Caribbean, Latin American history.
Deward Walker: Acculturation and cultural change, anthropology of education, cultural and environmental impact studies, ethnographic reconstruction and description.
William King: Afro-American studies; urban studies; citizenship and public affairs; science, technology and society.
David Naguib Pellow: Environmental sociology, qualitative/historical methods, race and ethnicity, work and occupations, social movements.

AFRICAN AMERICAN STUDIES

Brown University
Afro-American Studies Program
Box 1904, Churchill House
155 Angell Street, 2nd Floor
Providence, RI 02912
Phone: 401-863-3137
Email: *sheila_grant@brown.edu*
Web site: *www.brown.edu/departments/african_american_studies/*
Degree: B.A.

The Afro-American Studies program at Brown University focuses on theoretical, historical, and artistic exploration of the culture, philosophy, and literature of the Afro-Americas, including historic and present linkages to continental Africa. The concentration requires completion of at least eight courses in Afro-American studies. Students are expected to gain familiarity with the various disciplinary perspectives and geographic areas covered in the program's offerings. Concentrators are also required to elect at least six courses in one department of arts, sciences, or humanities in order to develop disciplinary as well as interdisciplinary competency, and are strongly urged to develop foreign language skills. The program encourages foreign study, preferably during the junior year. At least six courses offered for the concentration must, however, be completed in the program at Brown. A senior honors thesis option is available.

COURSE HIGHLIGHTS: Women, the State, and Violence/The City in Africa/Afro-American History and Society before 1800/ History, Nation, Popular Culture, and Caribbean Politics/Public Health in Africa: History, Politics, and Practice/West African History.

SELECTED FACULTY

Anani Dzidzienyo: Blacks in Latin American history, Afro-Brazilians and the Brazilian polity, comparative politics of Africa and Latin America.

Paget Henry: Dependency theory, Caribbean political economy, sociology of religion, Africana philosophy and religion, race and ethnic relations, critical theory.

Nancy Jacobs: Environmental history of Africa with a focus on southern Africa.

Joy James: African American social and political thought, Black feminist thought, critical race theory, urban politics, Cuban politics, the prison industrial complex.

University of North Carolina
Department of African and Afro-American Studies
109 Battle Hall, CB# 3395
Chapel Hill, NC 27599-3395
Phone: 919-966-5496
Fax: 919-962-2694
Email: *dacrowde@email.unc.edu*
Web site: *www.unc.edu/depts/afriafam/*
Degree: B.A.

The Department of African and Afro-American Studies is devoted to the study of the histories, cultures, and cultural linkages of the peoples of Africa and their descendants in the New World. The department, in cooperation with UNC's Institute for African American Research and Sonja Haynes Stone Black Cultural Center, sponsors a host of public outreach activities, including film and lecture series, teacher workshops, and service learning opportunities. Although students must concentrate in either African or Afro-American studies, all majors must gain competence in both areas and thereby come to understand the cultural and historical continuities and contrasts between Africa and the

African New World. Ten courses and proficiency in a modern foreign language are required for either concentration.

COURSE HIGHLIGHTS: Resistance Movements and Nationalism in Africa/Contemporary Africa: Issues in Health, Population, and the Environment/Blacks in Latin America/The Black Press and US History/African American Bioethics/Ethnography of Africa.

SELECTED FACULTY

Roberta Ann Dunbar: African social history, Muslim and civil law in francophone West Africa, comparative studies of gender and Islam in sub-Saharan Africa.

Gerald Horne: Progressive and protest movements in African American history, class issues, US foreign policy in Africa.

Tim McMillan: Colonialism in East Africa and the United States, African diaspora religions.

Catharine Newbury: Comparative politics and the political economy of development, women and development in the Third World, politics of agrarian change.

NATIVE AMERICAN STUDIES

University of Arizona
American Indian Studies Programs
430 Harvill Hall
Tucson AZ 85721-0076
Phone: 520-621-7108
Email: *aisp@u.arizona.edu*
Web site: *w3.arizona.edu/~aisp*
Degrees: M.A., J.D./M.A., Ph.D.

The University of Arizona's Graduate Interdisciplinary Program in American Indian Studies (AISP) seeks to develop, through research and scholarship, a wider scope of understanding of the indigenous peoples of the Americas—their languages, culture, traditions, and sovereignty. The program fosters interaction and supports productive scholarly activities with American Indian communities throughout the country. The master's program offers opportunities for advanced study in the concentrations of American Indian law and policy, American Indian societies and cultures, American Indian languages and literatures, and American Indian education. A concurrent Juris Doctorate and Master's degree will be granted upon the completion of a minimum of 106 units in law and American Indian studies. Graduates will be qualified to provide legal representation to Indian tribes, tribal organizations, and individuals in cases involving civil rights, land and water litigation, fishing and hunting rights, religious and cultural protections, and taxation of Indian lands. The joint degree takes four years to complete. In 1997, the university became the first educational institution in the US to offer a Ph.D. in American Indian studies.

COURSE HIGHLIGHTS: Ecology, Demography, and Disease/ Colonization and Native Peoples/Ethnology of Southwest/ American Indians and the Supreme Court/History of American Indian Education/The Anthropology of Visual Art/Studies in Oral Tradition/Folklore.

SELECTED FACULTY
Manley Begay: Nation building, curriculum development, indigenous education.
Robert Alan Hershey: Indigenous human rights, economic development in Indian country, criminal law in tribal courts, intellectual property rights.
Eileen Luna: Growth and development of tribal police, evaluation of human service delivery programs on Indian lands, community policing and disciplining the police.

Barbara Mills: Southwest archaeology, ceramic analysis, craft specialization, gender and archaeology, archaeology of inequality, ethnoarchaeology.

University of Kansas
Indigenous Nations Studies
215 Fraser Hall
Lawrence, KS 66045
Phone: 785-864-2660
Fax: 785-864-0370
Email: *insp@raven.cc.ukans.edu*
Web site: *www.ku.edu/~insp*
Degree: M.A.

Founded in 1997, the Indigenous Nations Studies program at the University of Kansas offers an interdisciplinary master's degree in the study of indigenous peoples throughout the Americas. The program prepares graduate students for academic and research careers and for leadership and policymaking roles in indigenous communities, higher education, and nonprofit organizations. Students pursuing the M.A. must take a minimum of thirty credit hours of coursework at the graduate level; fifteen to eighteen hours are to be completed in the student's designated study track. Three tracks are available: general, museum, and sovereignty development studies. The first track develops critical thinking and understanding of the cultural, economic, environmental, linguistic, political, and social needs of indigenous nations; the second trains professionals for positions in institutions responsible for collecting and studying the material record of the natural and cultural world; the third prepares students for the practical challenges associated with exercising indigenous rights of self-determination and the preservation and strengthening of tribal sovereignty. To complete the degree, students may write a thesis, perform six credit hours of classroom instruction, or participate in a supervised apprenticeship in an approved organization or setting related to indigenous peoples of the Americas.

COURSE HIGHLIGHTS: Sovereignty, Self-Determination, and Indigenous Nations/Native and Western Views of Nature/ Geography of American Indians/The Colonial Experience/ Economic Development of Latin America/Seminar in Archaeology: The Paleoindian New World.

SELECTED FACULTY

Bartholomew Dean: Anthropology, critical theory, kinship, politics, exchange, symbolic forms, social change and development, Amazonia, Latin America.
Donald Fixico: American Indian history, indigenous nations studies, policy studies, ethnohistory, oral history.
Joane Nagel: American Indian activism, politics, and policy; comparative ethnicity; race, gender, and sexuality.
Cornel Pewewardy: American Indian education, educational policy and theory, critical pedagogy, multicultural education.

GEOGRAPHY

University of Arizona
Department of Geography and Regional Development
409 Harvill Building, Box #2
Tucson, AZ 85721-0076
Phone: 520-621-1652
Fax: 520-621-2889
Email: *koski@geog.Arizona.edu*
Web site: *geog.arizona.edu/~web/*
Degrees: B.A., B.S., M.A., Ph.D.

The Department of Geography and Regional Development at the University of Arizona offers training at the bachelor's, master's, and doctoral levels. The faculty maintain broad teaching and research interests, including cultural-historical, economic, medical, nature-society relations, political, population and urban geography, physical geography (especially biogeography, climatology, and geomorphology), regional development, geographic information systems (GIS) and remote sensing, Anglo-America, arid lands, Latin America, the former Soviet Union, and the Middle East.

The M.A. degree is designed as a two-year program of study (minimum of 36 units). Students elect either a thesis option (recommended for those pursuing a Ph.D.) or a non-thesis option (recommended for those pursuing a professional, nonacademic career in GIS, regional development, etc.) At the master's level, the department offers specialized tracks in critical human geography, physical geography, and regional development, or a more general program tailored to the student's needs. The Ph.D. is a research-oriented degree requiring a qualifying examination (waived for students who meet certain minimum requirements), at least one year of coursework (minimum of 18 credits) in addition to the master's degree, and approximately three years of independent study and research culminating in the dissertation.

COURSE HIGHLIGHTS: The Middle Eastern City and Islamic Urbanism/Land Use and Growth Controls/Health and the Global Economy/Global Agricultural and International Relations/ Geography and Social Justice/Sustainable Cities and Societies.

SELECTED FACULTY

Michael Bonine: Middle East, arid lands, urban geography, human geography.

Adrian X. Esparza: City systems and services, information economy, urban-rural land use, inner-city revitalization.

George Henderson: Historical and cultural US, social theory, political economy of landscape and representation.

Diana Liverman: Human dimensions of global change, environmental policy and impact in Latin America.

University of California, Berkeley
Department of Geography
507 McCone Hall
Berkeley, CA 94720-4740
Phone: 510-642-3903
Fax: 510-642-3370
Email: *cgpage@socrates.berkeley.edu*
Web site: *geography.berkeley.edu*
Degrees: B.A., M.A., Ph.D.

The Geography Department at the University of California, Berkeley provides a broad-ranging perspective on the human transformation of the face of the earth. It offers undergraduate and graduate training for future scholars and teachers at the collegiate level, as well as for those going into professional careers in government, consulting, and nongovernmental organizations. The undergraduate major includes the study of various aspects of cultural, human, physical, and regional geography as well as cartography, quantitative methods, and fieldwork. Majors take three lower-division and at least eight upper-division courses; five of the latter must be in one specialty group. Specialty options are physical, development/environment, local/global, and methodology. High-achieving students may apply to the honors program, for which a thesis is required.

Students pursuing the Master of Arts degree select either Plan I, requiring a thesis, or Plan II, requiring an examination. Because students begin graduate studies with often widely different backgrounds—some have done much work in geography, some a little, while others have done none—the M.A. requirements will vary from student to student. All, however, must complete a foreign language requirement and develop a regional focus. Faculty will evaluate each student's overall performance upon completion of the master's and submit a recommendation as to whether the

Ph.D. should be pursued. Doctoral candidates must fulfill post-M.A. coursework and the Ph.D. language requirement before advancing to the oral examinations and dissertation.

COURSE HIGHLIGHTS: Ecological and Social Dimensions of Global Change/Nationalism, Identity, and Territoriality in Europe/Topics in Political Geography/Africa: Ecology and Development/Economic Geography of the Industrial World/ The Cultures of Cities.

SELECTED FACULTY

Orman Granger: Applied physical climatology, water resources, the environmental and economic impact of climatic change, geophysical hazards, the Caribbean.

Gillian Hart: Political economy of development, gender, agrarian and regional studies, labor, South Africa.

Allen Pred: Situated practices and everyday life, modern and historical geography of the present, the cultural reworking of global economic restructuring, Sweden and Europe.

Richard Walker: Economic geography, regional development, cities and urbanization, US, especially California and the San Francisco Bay Area, politics and theory.

Michael Watts: Third World political economy, political ecology, Africa, development, peasant societies, social and cultural theory, American agriculture.

University of Kentucky
Department of Geography
1457 Patterson Office Tower
Lexington, KY 40506-0027
Phone: 859-257-2931
Fax: 859-323-1969
Email (undergraduate): *brunn@pop.uky.edu*
Email (graduate): *geg207@pop.uky.edu*
Web site: *www.uky.edu/artssciences/geography/*
Degrees: B.A., M.A., Ph.D.

The University of Kentucky's Department of Geography has been identified as one of the best departments in human geography and among the most productive in terms of faculty research and publication. At the graduate level, the department emphasizes theoretical and methodological training; faculty and student research focuses on interrelated thematic clusters. Seminars are organized around topics relevant to these clusters; content varies in accordance with the current interests of faculty and graduate students. Opportunities exist for off-campus fieldwork, including summer field courses in Japan and Mexico.

The department maintains a commitment to quality undergraduate education. Students have opportunities for formal class contact with all faculty members, and an essentially open-door policy prevails in regard to undergraduate advising. The major is structured around a set of core courses, but students have the opportunity to design a focused curriculum by including relevant courses in both geography and related disciplines.

The University of Kentucky's Committee on Social Theory is concerned with building theoretical bridges between the humanities and social sciences and with exploring the consequences of theoretical and empirical research. Central thematic foci of the program include metropolises, children at the millennium, nation theory, revisioning ecological-social justice, whiteness, and contemporary democracy and democratic theory. Components of the program include a graduate certificate in social theory (open both to post-bachelor's student's and those pursuing a disciplinary degree), a distinguished author in social theory in the fall, a public lecture series coordinated with a team-taught graduate seminar, a student-edited journal (*disClosure*), community outreach and the opportunity to work with community organizations, and a working papers series.

COURSE HIGHLIGHTS: Sustainable Resource Development and Environmental Management/Geography of Information and Communications/Theories of Development and Anti-

Development/Issues in Contemporary Restructuring and Post-Communism.

SELECTED FACULTY

Oliver Fröhling: Social theory, political ecology, development and indigenous people, GIS, Mexico, Latin America, North America.
John Paul Jones III: Intersection of spatial theory and theories of identity, representation, and democracy.
John Pickles: Geographic thought and social theory, philosophy of science, regional development, transition theory and democratization, Africa, Eastern Europe.
Susan Roberts: Geography of financial capital; development, social, and feminist theory; global political economy; the Caribbean.

University of Minnesota
Department of Geography
414 Social Sciences Building
267 19th Avenue South
Minneapolis, MN 55455
Phone: 612-625-6080
Fax: 612-624-1044
Email: *geog@geog.umn.edu*
Web site: *www.geog.umn.edu*
Degrees: B.A., B.S., M.A., MGIS, Ph.D.

At the University of Minnesota's Department of Geography, under-graduate majors may earn either a B.A. with a focus in city systems or regional analysis and development, or a B.S. in environmental systems or geographic information, analysis, and representation. For both degrees, three core courses, a modes of geographic inquiry course, and four or five track courses are required, as is a senior project.

The department offers three graduate degree programs: the M.A. and Ph.D. in geography and the MGIS (Master of Geographic Information Science). The master's and doctorate in geography are academic, or research, degrees: many students in the master's program continue into the Ph.D. program; most students in the Ph.D. program are preparing for academic careers. The MGIS professional degree does not lead to admission to a Ph.D. program, but prepares students in the theoretical, technical, and applied aspects of geographic information science.

Undergraduates, graduates, and faculty have access to extensive resources in the department and across the university to support their geographic research. These range from tools and data, to collaboration through research centers, support for ethical research practices, and institutional administration of funded projects.

COURSE HIGHLIGHTS: The State, the Economy, and Spatial Development/Geographical Analysis of Environmental Systems and Global Change/Geography of Health and Health Care/ Geographical Perspectives on Planning/Population in an Interacting World.

SELECTED FACULTY

Bruce Braun: Society-environment relations, political ecology, social and cultural theory, cultural studies of the environment, colonial and post-colonial geographies.

Helga Leitner: Urban and political geography, international migrations, social theory, GIS and society, Europe and the European Union.

Earl P. Scott: Human landscape geography, small-scale enterprise and economic development, Africa, minority settlements in the US with emphasis on the African diaspora.

Eric Sheppard: Economic geography, environmental justice, geography of development, urban systems change, telecommunications and geography.

Syracuse University
Department of Geography
144 Eggers Hall
Syracuse University

Syracuse, NY 13244-1020
Phone: 315-443-2605
Fax: 315-443-4227
Email: *cmchapma@maxwell.syr.edu*
Web site: *www.maxwell.syr.edu/geo/indexgeo.htm*
Degrees: B.A., M.A., Ph.D.

Syracuse University's Geography Department makes every effort to foster a close and open working relationship between students and faculty. Students at all levels are expected to participate in activities outside of formal classes; the department sponsors a weekly colloquium, student seminars, and visiting lectures, among other activities. The standard M.A. program consists of 30 hours of approved graduate credit, at least half of which must be at the 600 level or above. Courses and requirements depend on the student's interests and academic objectives; emphasis is placed on the acquisition of a range of research skills and methods that can be applied in a variety of career contexts and used in doctoral programs. The Ph.D. program calls for an additional 30 credit hours of courses either inside or outside the department, the writing of an approved dissertation proposal, satisfactory completion of a combined written and oral qualifying examination, and finally, successful completion of the dissertation. Students wishing to enter the doctoral program should have a reasonably clear idea of dissertation plans to facilitate construction of a doctoral program of study. All applicants are encouraged to correspond with individual faculty regarding their special interest in any aspect of the Syracuse program in geography.

The geography major consists of a minimum of 30 credit hours, or ten courses. After completing foundation work on the natural environment and world cultures, the student must choose at least seven upper-division courses from a wide array of systematic and regional topics. A senior-year proseminar requirement ensures that the student pursues a particular research topic in some depth and is able to present and justify his or her findings in both oral and

written form. Simultaneous participation in the honors program is
encouraged, and numerous possibilities also exist for dual majors.

COURSE HIGHLIGHTS: Geopolitics in Theory and Practice/
China: Geography and Political Economy/Global Economic
Geography/The New North Americas/Science, Society, and
Environmental Conflict/Urban Historical Geography/Geography
and the Internet.

SELECTED FACULTY

Don Mitchell: Production and meaning of public space, theory
and historical study of landscape, historical geography of science.
Anne Mosher: Industrial restructuring and labor, resource
communities and company towns, place commodification and
tourism, built environment and cultural landscape.
Beverly Mullings: Globalization and industrial change in
developing countries; international trade in services; women,
work, and industrial change.
John Rennie Short: Urban development, political economy of
cities, urban social theory, cultural representation of
environment, environmental ideology.

University of Washington
Department of Geography
Box 353550
Seattle, WA 98195-3550
Phone: 206-543-5843
Fax: 206-543-3313
Email: *geog@u.washington.edu*
Web site: *depts.washington.edu/geog*
Degrees: B.A., M.A., Ph.D.

The Department of Geography at the University of Washington
offers highly regarded programs for both graduates and undergraduates. Its formal emphases are urban, social and political geography; economic geography; regional geography and international

development studies; geographic information systems (GIS); and society and environment. At the graduate level, the master's degree normally takes two years to complete, and the doctorate, three additional years. Degree programs are highly individualized and unstructured in order to accommodate the interests of the individual student. In addition to one or two foundation courses, all students must take at least two methods courses (GIS analysis, qualitative reasoning, quantitative reasoning, etc.) and graduate research seminars. Doctoral students are also required to have either a professional publication in a refereed journal or have applied for a nationally competitive research fellowship.

Undergraduates choose from among five concentrations and complete a capstone experience, which may include a senior essay, seminars, or workshops. A number of undergraduate courses carry a service-learning component, in which students participate in volunteer work connected to the course content and then synthesize theory with practice in written projects.

COURSE HIGHLIGHTS: Consumption, Nature, and Globalization/ Migration in the Global Economy/Geopolitics/ Gender, Race, and the Geography of Employment/Critical and Normative Ecologies/Industrialization and Urbanization in China.

SELECTED FACULTY

Lucy Jarosz: Geography of food and agriculture, environmental and landscape change, development theory, Africa.

Nayna Jhaveri: Nature-society relations; postmodern ecology; geography of consumption, common property; critical environmental law; water resources; Asia.

Katharyne Mitchell: Cultural and economic geography, the urban environment, migration and capital flows between the Pacific Rim and the Pacific Northwest, social theory.

Matthew Sparke: Critical geopolitics, political and economic geography, social theory including post-colonial theory and feminist and anti-racist theory, US and Canada.

HISTORY

University of California, Los Angeles
Department of History
6265 Bunche Hall
Box 951473
Los Angeles, CA 90095-1473
Phone: 310-825-4601
Email (undergraduate): *padilla@history.ucla.edu*
Email (graduate): *patel@history.ucla.edu*
Web site: *www.sscnet.ucla.edu/history/*
Degrees: B.A., Ph.D.

The Department of History at UCLA offers the following graduate fields of study: Africa, Near East, East Asia (China and Japan), South and Southeast Asia, history of religion, history of science, Latin America, the United States, and Europe (ancient, Jewish, medieval, and modern). Degree requirements vary from field to field. The department grants only the Ph.D.; terminal master's degrees are not available. Full-time attendance is necessary, as classes are held during the day. Prior to formal application, prospective students are encouraged to start an email dialogue with one or two faculty members in their field of specialization. At least one faculty member must be interested in working with the student.

At the undergraduate level, students take two courses each in introductory, United States, European, and non-Western history. Students must also complete a course in historical practice, and in their senior year they undertake one piece of sustained research in a focused historical subject. Outside of the requirements, students are free to follow their interests.

COURSE HIGHLIGHTS: American Working Class Movements/ Culture and Power in Late Imperial China/Social Theory and Comparative History/Native American Revitalization

Movements/Global Economic Integration, 1200–1800/Europe
and the World: Colonialism, Slavery, and Revolution, 1700–1870.

SELECTED FACULTY

Robert Brenner: Early modern European history; economic,
social, and religious history; agrarian history; social theory/
Marxism; Tudor-Stuart England.

John H.M. Laslett: US labor and social movements; US, Asian,
Black, and Mexican immigration; comparative Euro-American
history.

Geoffrey Robinson: Early and modern Southeast Asia; political
violence, genocide, and human rights.

Michael Salman: Philippine history, comparative history of
slavery and abolition, imperialism.

University of California, Santa Cruz
Department of History
1156 High Street
Santa Cruz, CA 95064-1077
Phone (undergraduate): 831-459-2982
Phone (graduate): 831-459-4192
Fax: 831-459-3125
Email (undergraduate): *sshinkle@cats.ucsc.edu*
Email (graduate): *diane@cats.ucsc.edu*
Web site: *humwww.ucsc.edu/academic.html*
Degrees: B.A., M.A., Ph.D.

The Ph.D. program in history at the University of California, Santa
Cruz emphasizes an interdisciplinary and cross-cultural approach
to historical studies. All applicants to the Ph.D. program apply for
admission to a specific thematic cluster as well as to the program
as a whole. The department currently offers four basic groupings:
colonialism, nationalism and race; the history of gender; society
and culture; culture, society, and power in the early modern world.
In preparing graduate students for research and teaching at the
university level, the department also offers training in four geo-

graphically defined teaching fields: US history, European history since 1500, East Asian history since 1600, and world history since 1500. Each student selects a primary and secondary field. The M.A. degree is awarded to all students after two years in residence, successful completion of 12 courses and a substantial research essay (25–30 pages), and for those in primary teaching fields other than US history, demonstrated competence in one foreign language. Before beginning the dissertation, students must prepare a dossier and pass a three-hour qualifying examination in their research field, outside (nonhistory) field, and two teaching fields.

Undergraduates must choose from among three geographic areas of concentration (the Americas; Europe; or Asia/Africa/the Middle East/World) and complete at least twelve courses for the major. A senior comprehensive is required, either in the form of a seminar or thesis.

COURSE HIGHLIGHTS: Race and the Intimacies of Empire/ Making the Mediterranean Modern, 1750–1950/Engendering China/Intellectual and Social History of Modern India/Fascism and Resistance in Italy/Tale of Two Cities: Los Angeles and Mexico.

SELECTED FACULTY

Edmund Burke III: Islamic history, modern Middle Eastern and North African history, French history, European imperialism, world history.

Gail Hershatter: Modern Chinese social and cultural history, labor history, women's history, history of sexuality, feminist theory; history, memory, and nostalgia.

David G. Sweet: Social, cultural, and environmental history of colonial and modern Latin America and Southeast Asia; Native and African experience in colonial America.

Mark Traugott: Social and economic history of 19th-century France, French revolutions, European working-class historical methods, workers' autobiographies.

Columbia University

Department of History
Mail Code 2527
611 Fayerweather Hall
New York, NY 10027
Phone: 212-854-4646
Fax: 212-932-0602
Email (graduate): *keo7@columbia.edu*
Email (undergraduate): *jrl100@columbia.edu*
Web site: *www.columbia.edu/cu/history/*
Degrees: B.A., M.A., Ph.D.

Columbia University's graduate program in history offers the fields of African, ancient, early modern European, East Asian, Jewish, Latin American, medieval, Middle Eastern, modern Western European, East Central European, Russian, South Asian, and United States history, as well as the history of public health. In their first two years, students take coursework and prepare for oral exams; in the third year and beyond, students complete their oral exams, then write and defend the dissertation prospectus and dissertation. Most students also become involved in teaching to some degree beginning in the second or third year—at Columbia, Barnard, or elsewhere. The department admits a limited number of students to its terminal master's degree program; many pursue the degree on a part-time basis.

Undergraduate majors fulfill a minimum of 29 credits in history, ten within their field of specialization and nine outside it. Two seminars are also required, and a senior thesis option is available. Students may arrange independent reading courses with individual faculty.

COURSE HIGHLIGHTS: Modern American Social Movements/ History of the City of New York/Disease, Public Health, and Empire/Poverty and Social Order in Europe/Colonial Encounters/ History of Development in Africa Since 1945/Mexican Politics in the 20th Century.

SELECTED FACULTY

Eric Foner: Civil War and Reconstruction, slavery, 19th-century America.

Ira Katznelson: American politics, comparative politics, political theory, urban politics, race relations, class formation, education, urban geography, social movements.

Alice Kessler-Harris: History of American labor, comparative and interdisciplinary study of women and gender.

Manning Marable: African American history.

Duke University
Department of History
Box 90719
Durham, NC 27708
Phone (undergraduate): 919-684-2409
Phone (graduate): 919-681-5746
Web site: *www.history.aas.duke.edu*
Degrees: B.A., M.A., Ph.D.

Duke University's History Department offers the Bachelor of Arts, Master of Arts, and Doctor of Philosophy degrees. Most graduate students are admitted for the Ph.D. degree, but each year some are admitted, without university funding, to pursue an M.A. The master's degree can be completed in three semesters, or in twelve months by those who choose to attend summer session. While the doctorate can be completed in four years, it usually takes five to six years. Duke frequently accepts students with master's degrees from other schools, or master's degrees in other fields. M.A. candidates satisfy requirements in coursework, written work, and foreign language proficiency, and participate in an informal exam, or Master's Meeting. A thesis is not required. Candidates for the doctorate are required to prepare four general preliminary examination fields.

History majors concentrate their work in a primary field, which can be either a geographic region or a thematic area. Reflecting current department strengths, recognized thematic areas are the history of the African diaspora; the history of medicine, science, and technology; the history of women; and military history. Students may define other thematic areas, with approval of the director of undergraduate studies and the student's advisor.

COURSE HIGHLIGHTS: War, Revolution, and Society in the Caribbean, 1700–1815/Social Conflict in Weimar and Nazi Germany/Culture of American Capitalism, 1750–1860/Labor Systems in African History/Working Class in the United States.

SELECTED FACULTY
Arif Dirlik: History of Modern China with emphasis on social, political, and historical thinking.
Janet Ewald: History of Africa with special focus on Islamic Africa, comparative slavery, and historical methodology for nonliterate societies.
John D. French: Labor and politics in twentieth-century Latin America with special emphasis on Brazil.
Alexander Keyssar: Late 19th- and 20th-century US history, including labor and working class history; political and economic history; history of institutions.

University of Michigan
Department of History
1029 Tisch Hall
555 South State Street
Ann Arbor, MI 48109-1003
Phone: 734-764-6305
Fax: 734-647-4881
Email: *umhistory@umich.edu*
Web site: *www.lsa.umich.edu/history*
Degrees: B.A., Ph.D.

The Department of History at the University of Michigan offers degrees at the graduate and undergraduate levels. Undergraduates concentrating in the field take two introductory, eight major, and two cognate (related but nonhistory) courses. Graduate students fulfill course, seminar, and cognate requirements and pass the written and oral general examination before proceeding to the dissertation. Ph.D. candidates are generally enrolled for four to six terms. A comprehensive range of geographical/chronological and topical fields are available for graduate study.

The university maintains a strong commitment to inter-disciplinary research. Its Program in the Comparative Study of Social Transformations (CSST) seeks to link the study of social transformations with the intellectual transformations that accompany them, and with theoretical shifts in scholarly thought. With the participation of over 130 faculty from numerous disciplines, CSST organizes public colloquia, faculty and graduate student symposia, and conferences, and produces a working paper series.

COURSE HIGHLIGHTS: New Worlds: Colonialism and Cultural Encounters/Health and Illness in African Worlds/Law, Race, and Citizenship: Cuba and the US/Mapping Arabia/Institutions of Social Memory/Agrarian Questions: Peasants, Power, and Transitions to and from Capitalism/History and Domestic Policymaking.

SELECTED FACULTY

Fernando Coronil: Historical anthropology, state formation, capitalism, popular culture, gender; Latin America.

Geoff Eley: The European left, 1848 to the present; German liberalism, 1848 to 1933; conceptions of class in history and politics; nationalism, fascism, and state formation.

Gabrielle Hecht: History of technology; France; Africa; colonialism and post-coloniality; labor; national identity.

Nancy Hunt: Africa, women's history, history of medicine.

William G. Rosenberg: Imperial Russia and the Soviet Union; revolutionary movements; labor, intellectual, and religious history.

Northwestern University
Department of History
Harris Hall, Room 202
Evanston, IL 60208-2220
Phone: 847-491-2846
Fax: 847-467-1393
Web site: *www2.mmlc.nwu.edu/history*
Degrees: B.A., Ph.D.

Northwestern University's Department of History offers the Ph.D. in the main regional concentrations of US, European, and African history. Only fifteen to twenty applicants are admitted to the program each year. Each student's flexible course of study revolves around three chosen fields: general, minor, and specialization. The general field is the general area of research training; the specialization is the dissertation sub-field; and the minor is a field of teaching competence, or methodological or topical interest. In addition to coursework, the doctorate requires up to three foreign languages (as relevant), oral and substantive examinations in all three fields, and the dissertation. Interdisciplinary strengths at Northwestern include African studies, economic history, women's history, medieval and renaissance culture, and modern Europe.

Students majoring in history select one of four concentrations: history of the Americas, English/European history, African/Middle Eastern history, or Asian/Middle Eastern history. The program consists of eleven graded quarter-courses in history and five graded quarter-courses in related subjects. An honors thesis option is available.

COURSE HIGHLIGHTS: On the Margins: Outside the Mainstream in the Middle Ages/Revolution in 20th-Century Latin America/Social and Cultural History of Colonial America/Comparative Method and African History/Development of the Modern American City.

SELECTED FACULTY

Steven Hahn: Nineteenth-century US social and political history, particularly popular politics in the south.

Laura Hein: History of Japan in the 20th century and its international relations.

E. William Monter: Early modern social history, witchcraft, the Inquisition, women's history, perceived deviance.

David Schoenbrun: African history before the 16th century and in nontraditional sources for writing history.

University of Wisconsin
Department of History
3211 Humanities Building
455 North Park Street
Madison, WI 53706
Phone: 608-263-1800
Fax: 608-263-5302
Email: *history@ls.admin.wisc.edu*
Web site: *history.wisc.edu/index.htm*
Degrees: B.A., M.A., Ph.D.

The University of Wisconsin's Department of History offers graduate programs leading to the M.A. and Ph.D. degrees. Some departmental regulations and requirements apply to all students, while others touch only individual study programs, offered in American, European, African, Central Asian, East Asian, Latin American, Middle Eastern, South Asian, and Southeast Asian history. The faculty in the study programs define each field's requirements and compose its preliminary examinations. Specific requirements for coursework, languages, and examinations vary by program of study.

The undergraduate history major requires a minimum of thirty credits, at least half of which must be in advanced-level coursework. Students must take at least one course each in US, European, and Third World history, and at least one of the foregoing must be in ancient or medieval history. An honors program and a thesis option are available.

COURSE HIGHLIGHTS: Seminar in the Social History of Modern Europe/Mexican Revolution: Background, Development, and Consequences/Comparative History of Education in Colonial Societies/Islamic History From the Origin of Islam to the Ottoman Empire/Race, Class, and Colonialism in the Caribbean.

SELECTED FACULTY

Jeanne Boydston: US women's history; US history 1798–1850; gender, labor, and the transition to capitalism; gay/lesbian US history.

Suzanne Desan: Early modern France, especially the French Revolution; popular politics; women's activism; rural communities; French revolutionary symbols and culture.

Florencia Mallon: Latin American history, especially Mexico, Peru, and Chile; agrarian history; social movements; popular culture; social theory; women's history; ethnicity.

Thomas Spear: Pre-colonial African history, historical methods and theory, social and economic history of Africa, ethnicity, religious movements, resistance, agriculture.

Yale University
Department of History
PO Box 208324
New Haven, CT 06520-8324
Phone: 203-432-1363
Email (graduate): *john.demos@yale.edu*
Email (undergraduate): *paul.freedman@yale.edu*
Web site: *www.yale.edu/history*
Degrees: B.A., M.A., M.Phil., Ph.D.

Yale University's Department of History boasts faculty strength across a broad spectrum of geographical and topical fields. During the first two years of graduate study, students normally take twelve term courses, at least eight of which shall be chosen from those offered by the department. Three of the twelve courses must be research seminars, and one of the second-year courses will be a tutorial resulting in a prospectus for the dissertation. All students must pass examinations in at least two foreign languages, one by the end of the first year. In the third year, students take an oral examination in three chosen fields of concentration. Qualification for admission to candidacy for the Ph.D. must take place by the end of the third year of study. A terminal M.A. is available, as is a Master of Philosophy degree for those who have completed all requirements for Ph.D. candidacy.

For the major, undergraduates must take 12 terms of history in all, including two terms of US or Canadian history, two terms of European or British history, and three terms of African, Asian, Latin American, or Middle East history. Two of the seven specified terms must be courses in pre-industrial history from two of the foregoing categories. Junior seminars and a senior departmental essay are also required.

COURSE HIGHLIGHTS: Spain's North American Borderlands/ Empires and Imperialisms/Agrarian Societies/Consumer Culture in Historical Perspective/Social History of the Chinese Silk Routes/ Political Theory and Practice in Persian Historical Texts and Contexts.

SELECTED FACULTY

Jennifer Baszile: African American history before 1865, early North America, comparative colonialism.
Gilbert Joseph: Agrarian history, Mexican history, Latin American social and cultural history.
Benedict Kiernan: History of Southeast Asia, history of genocide.
Michael Mahoney: Social and cultural history of Africa from 1800 to the present.

Also recommended

University of California, Santa Barbara
Department of History
Santa Barbara, CA 93106-9410
Phone: 805-893-2991
Fax: 805-893-8795
Email (undergraduate): *tucker@humanitas.ucsb.edu*
Email (graduate): *isono@humanitas.ucsb.edu*
Web site: *www.history.ucsb.edu*
Degrees: B.A., M.A., Ph.D.

GRADUATE FIELDS OF STUDY: Ancient Mediterranean World/
Medieval Europe/Early Modern Europe/Modern Europe/United
States/Latin American, Colonial Period/Latin American,
National Period/East Asia/Middle East/Africa/History of
Science/History of Public Policy.

University of Illinois, Urbana-Champaign
309 Gregory Hall
810 South Wright Street
Urbana, IL 61801
Phone: 217-333-1155
Fax: 217-333-2297
Email (undergraduate): *mblocher@uiuc.edu*
Email (graduate): *judyp@uiuc.edu*
Web site: *www.history.uiuc.edu*
Degrees: B.A., Ph.D.

GRADUATE FIELDS OF STUDY: Africa/Afro-American/
American Intellectual and Cultural/Britain and Empire–
Commonwealth since 1688/British Isles to 1688/Colonial North
America and Early US to 1830/Colonialism and Post-Colonialism/
Comparative Labor and Working Class/Cultural and Intellectual/
East Asia/Eastern and Southeastern Europe/Europe 1648–1789/

Europe since 1789/Greece/History of Medicine/History of
Nationalism/History of Science/History of Women and Gender/
Latin America/Middle Ages/Military History/Middle East/"Race,"
Ethnic Identity Formation, and Hybridity/Religion in Pre-Modern
Society/Renaissance and Reformation/Russia/United States
since 1830.

University of Illinois, Chicago
Department of History
913 University Hall
601 South Morgan Street
Chicago, IL 60607-7109
Phone: 312-996-3141
Fax: 312-996-6377
Email: *arnesen@uic.edu*
Web site: *www.uic.edu/depts/hist*
Degrees: B.A., M.A., Ph.D.

GRADUATE FIELDS OF STUDY, MASTER'S LEVEL: Africa/
Ancient World/Early Modern Europe/East Asia/Great Britain/
Latin America/Medieval Europe/Modern Europe/Russia and East
Europe/United States.

GRADUATE FIELDS OF STUDY, DOCTORAL LEVEL:
Africa/Britain since 1485/Europe 1450–1815/Europe since 1648/
France/Latin America/Russia/United States 1500–1877/United
States since 1765.

GRADUATE CONCENTRATIONS, THEMATIC: Gender and
women's studies; Latin American/Latino studies; history of work,
race, and gender in the urban world.

NOTED DEPARTMENTAL STRENGTHS: Gender and women's
history, American comparative labor and economic/business
history, African and African American history, urban history.

New York University
Department of History
53 Washington Square South
Seventh Floor
New York, NY 10012
Phone: 212-998-8600
Fax: 212-995-4017
Web site: *www.nyu.edu/gsas/dept/history*
Degrees: B.A., M.A., Ph.D.

GRADUATE FIELDS OF STUDY: African Diaspora/Atlantic
World/Europe from the Fall of Rome to the Fourteenth
Century/Europe 1400–1789/Europe 1750–present/Latin America
and the Caribbean/United States/Near East/Asia.

University of North Carolina, Chapel Hill
Department of History
Hamilton Hall, CB #3195
Chapel Hill, NC 27599-3195
Phone: 919-962-2115
Fax: 919-962-1403
Email: *history@unc.edu*
Web site: *www.unc.edu/depts/history*
Degrees: B.A., M.A., Ph.D.

GRADUATE FIELDS OF STUDY: Ancient/Europe/Latin America/
Russia and East Europe/United States/History of Women/History
of Science, Medicine, and Technology/Military History.

Northern Arizona University
Department of History
Liberal Arts, Box 6023
Flagstaff, AZ 86011
Phone: 520-523-4378
Fax: 520-523-1277

Email: *john.leung@nau.edu*
Web site: *www.nau.edu/~history*
Degrees: B.A., B.S., M.A., Ph.D.

GRADUATE FIELDS OF STUDY, GEOGRAPHIC: North America
(with a special emphasis on the American Southwest and
Borderlands)/Europe/ Latin America/Asia.

GRADUATE FIELDS OF STUDY, THEMATIC: Gender, Race, and
Class/Colonialism and Nationalism/Politics, Ideology, and
Conflict/Environment and Economy.

Rutgers University
Department of History
16 Seminary Place
New Brunswick, NJ 08901-1108
Phone: 732-932-7905
Fax: 732-932-6763
Email (undergraduate): *undergrad@history.rutgers.edu*
Email (graduate): *graduate@history.rutgers.edu*
Web site: *history.rutgers.edu*
Degrees: B.A., Ph.D.

GRADUATE FIELDS OF STUDY: United States (early, 19th- and
20th-century, African American)/Europe (medieval, early
modern, modern)/Latin America/East Asia (China, Japan)/
Transnational Concentrations (Comparative and Global History,
Women's and Gender History, History of Diplomacy and Foreign
Relations).

NOTED DEPARTMENTAL STRENGTHS: Social and cultural
history; women's and gender history; political and diplomatic
history; the history of technology, medicine, and science; Early
American history; African American history; comparative and
global history; Latin American history; modern Russian history.

HUMAN RIGHTS

Columbia University
Center for the Study of Human Rights
1108 International Affairs Building
420 West 118th Street
MC 3365
New York, NY 10027
Phone: 212-854-2479
Fax: 212-316-4578
Email: *cshr@columbia.edu*
Web site: *www.columbia.edu/cu/humanrights/index*
Degree: M.A.

Columbia University has possibly the most comprehensive set of academic programs in human rights studies in the country. Its School of International and Public Affairs (SIPA) offers a two-year master's degree in international affairs (MIA) with a concentration in human rights. The MIA Human Rights program is designed to prepare students for a wide range of non-legal careers concerned with human rights, such as policy and research, monitoring and peacekeeping, or NGO and governmental work. The one-year Liberal Studies M.A. in human rights, administered by the Graduate School of Arts and Sciences, is in contrast geared toward those in other fields for whom a knowledge of human rights principles and applications is useful: health, social work, education, politics, religion, or business. Students in the latter program choose from among four areas of concentration (health, women, communication, or economics and development) and may be enrolled full- or part-time.

Human rights courses, internships, and a student-run advocacy project are available to undergraduate students at Columbia College. Columbia Law School is home to a Human Rights

Institute sponsoring seminars, workshops, and a fellows program. A Human Rights Colloquium is open to doctoral students through the University's Center for the Study of Human Rights.

COURSE HIGHLIGHTS: Human Rights and Social Justice/ Constitutionalism in Comparative Perspective/Media and Human Rights Advocacy/Women, Religion, and Human Rights.

SELECTED FACULTY

Andrea Bartoli: International conflict resolution, religion and conflict resolution, conflict in sub-Saharan Africa.
Peter Juviler: Comparative politics, human rights situation in post-Soviet states.
Thomas Lansner: Media and human rights, sanctions and human rights, South and Southeast Asia (especially Burma), boycotts.
Andrew Nathan: Human rights in China.
Thomas Pogge: Ethics, concepts of global justice, political philosophy.

University of Denver

Graduate School of International Studies
2201 South Gaylord Street
Denver, CO 80208
Phone: 303-871-2544
Fax: 303-871-3585
Email: *gsisadm@du.edu*
Web site: *www.du.edu/humanrights*
Degree: M.A.

The Graduate School of International Studies (GSIS) offers a Master of Arts in international human rights (MIHP), emphasizing the integration of theory, policy analysis, and practice. Degree requirements consist of an international studies core, a human rights core, skills courses in statistical method and related topics, an internship, foreign language proficiency, and electives.

Opportunities for collateral coursework and joint degrees are plentiful at DU. Within GSIS, degree programs in international administration, public policy, and development offer numerous courses likely to be of interest to MIHP students. Joint degree programs in intercultural communications, law, management, and social work reflect well-established links with these professional schools, and the adjacent Iliff School of Theology has a large and active peace and justice program.

Through the Human Rights Advocacy Center, DU students in international studies, law, and other disciplines provide human rights attorneys and nongovernmental organizations in developing countries with *pro bono* research and consultative assistance. The GSIS student-run Center on Rights Development engages in a variety of information, outreach, and advocacy activities. These include publication of an electronic journal, *Globaljustice*, a speaker's series, and an annual human rights film festival.

COURSE HIGHLIGHTS: Human Rights and the International Refugee System/Peacekeeping/Comparative Genocide/The Future of Sovereignty.

SELECTED FACULTY

Jack Donnelly: Human rights and cultural relativism, human rights and development, humanitarian intervention.
Micheline Ishay: Human rights, political theory, international relations, comparative politics, nationalism.
Thomas Rowe: International peacekeeping, conflict and conflict resolution, human rights.

University of Dayton

Human Rights Program
Mark Ensalaco, Director
300 College Park
Dayton, OH 45469-1491
Phone: 937-229-2765
Fax: 937-229-2766

Email: *ensalaco@udayton.edu*
Web site: *www.as.udayton.edu/humanrightsprogram*
Degree: B.A.

In December 1998, the College of Arts and Sciences at the University of Dayton formally established a minor in human rights and incorporated a concentration in human rights into the existing international studies major program. These were the first undergraduate degree programs specifically concerned with human rights in the United States at that time. Both programs provide students with opportunities to address issues related to human rights from various disciplinary approaches.

The curriculum for students of international studies and human rights includes a core of courses in economics, history, and political science required of all majors; foreign language study; and a choice between area studies or global development concentrations. Majors are also required to incorporate an international and/or cross-cultural experimental component, of at least four weeks duration, into their program. Electives may be used to develop second majors or minors. The human rights minor requires at least nineteen credit hours to be taken from at least three different disciplines. At least twelve of these hours are to be taken outside one's major or majors. No more than six semester hours from any one department may be chosen from the elective pool. Courses taken from this minor may be applied to other minors and to breadth and general education requirements.

COURSE HIGHLIGHTS: Comparative Economic Systems/ Philosophy and Human Rights/Social Inequality/Social Justice in Latin America/International Social Work.

SELECTED FACULTY
Mark Ensalaco: Human rights policy with focus on South America.
Theo Majka: Issues of immigration, ethnicity, and community.
Michael Payne: Philosophy of law, social and political philosophy, ethics.

Trinity College
International Human Rights Program
Maryam Elahi, Director
300 Summit Street
Hartford, CT 06106-3100
Phone: 860-297-2437
Fax: 860-297-5108
Email: *maryam.elahi@trincoll.edu*
Web site: *www.trincoll.edu/depts/humanrights/*

Trinity College initiated its human rights minor in 1999. Participating students take five courses and an integrating exercise (which may be either an independent study or internship) and write a substantial paper. The interdisciplinary academic program is complemented with a lecture series, a visiting scholar/activist program, and fellowships for summer internship work with human rights advocacy organizations.

COURSE HIGHLIGHTS: International Human Rights Law and Advocacy/Human Rights: Philosophical Foundations, Issues, and Debates/Human Rights in a Global Age.

SELECTED FACULTY
Maryam Elahi: Human rights law.
Laurel Baldwin-Ragaven: Health and human rights, global women's health issues.
Michael Niemann: International relations with focus on southern Africa.
Maurice Wade: Human rights philosophy, racism, collective identity.

INTERNATIONAL STUDIES/INTERNATIONAL RELATIONS

University of Chicago
Center for International Studies
5828 South University Avenue
Chicago, IL 60637
Phone: 773-702-7721
Fax: 773-702-9286
Email: *v-beard@uchicago.edu*
Web site: *humanities.uchicago.edu/cis/*
Degree: B.A.

The Center for International Studies (CIS) at the University of Chicago is home to five federally funded National Resource Centers devoted to promoting the in-depth study of the language, history, and culture of specific regions of the world. CIS sponsors a Bachelor of Arts degree in international studies, drawing on existing strengths of the faculty in a variety of international fields and on innovative work in a number of CIS project areas, including human rights and globalization. All concentrators are required to take core classes, a two-quarter B.A. seminar, and ten courses from at least two of the four international studies sub-fields (international relations; international and comparative history; international political economy, business, and economics; and area and civilization studies). Language proficiency and overseas study are also compulsory.

COURSE HIGHLIGHTS: Religious Tradition/Politics of Gender/Military Theory and Practice/Problems in Human Geography: Middle East Colonial Servitude and Slavery/Amazonian Ethnography/Global Local Politics/Orientalism and Historiography.

SELECTED FACULTY

Arjun Appadurai: Ethnic violence, global cities, transnational civil formations.

Jacqueline Bhabha: Alien citizenship and rights, refugee law, human rights.

Rashid Khalidi: History of the modern Middle East, with an emphasis on the emergence of national identity and the involvement of external powers in the region.

University of Denver

Graduate School of International Studies
2201 South Gaylord Street
Denver, CO 80208
Phone: 303-871-2544
Fax: 303-871-3585
Email: *gsisadm@du.edu*
Web site: *www.du.edu/gsis*
Degrees: M.A., Ph.D.

Through the Graduate School of International Studies (GSIS) at the University of Denver, students may pursue graduate and undergraduate degrees. GSIS offers a traditional M.A. in international studies, several professional M.A. degrees directed at specific topical areas, and a Master of Public Policy. It also participates in dual and joint degree programs with other units of the University of Denver, including the Daniels College of Business, the College of Law, the School of Communication, and the Graduate School of Social Work. The 90-credit curriculum requires two years of full-time study, while dual degrees require three to four years, although particular curriculum requirements and application procedures may vary from program to program.

The topical Master of Arts programs include degrees in global finance, trade, and economic integration; technology and international public policy; international development; and global studies.

COURSE HIGHLIGHTS: Political Repression/Outbreak of War/ Global Inequality/Technology and Public Policy/Nonprofits/ Peacekeeping/Group and Organizational Dynamics/Economics of Underdevelopment/Contemporary Political Theory.

SELECTED FACULTY

George DeMartino: International economic integration, global political economy, environmental economics, labor economics, comparative labor systems.

Ilene Grabel: International finance, political economy, development and international economics, and finance and economic development.

David Goldfischer: Impact of globalization on international security, security and human rights.

John Grove: Comparative politics, nationalism, race and ethnicity, development, conflict resolution.

University of Southern California

School of International Relations
Von KleinSmid Center 330
3518 Trousdale Parkway
Los Angeles, CA 90089-0043
Phone: 213-740-6278
Fax: 213-742-0281
Email: *sir@usc.edu*
Web site: *www.usc.edu/dept/LAS/ir/*
Degrees: B.A., M.A., Ph.D.

The School of International Relations at the University of Southern California offers undergraduate courses leading to the Bachelor of Arts degree in international relations (IR) and graduate courses leading to the degrees of Master of Arts and Doctor of Philosophy. In addition, the Ph.D. in political economy and public policy is offered in cooperation with the Department of Economics and Political Science and the M.A./J.D. in conjunction with the USC Law Center.

The curriculum balances theoretical and policy-oriented knowledge. Undergraduates are encouraged to pursue double majors and may choose to write an honors thesis. A five-year B.A./M.A. plan is available. Unlike all but a handful of universities, USC offers masters and doctoral programs specifically in international relations rather than IR as a sub-field of political science. Fewer than thirty new students are admitted to the graduate program each year, resulting in a highly favorable faculty-student ratio. The School's Center for International Studies provides funding for students and visiting scholars, organizes seminars, and brings numerous speakers to campus.

COURSE HIGHLIGHTS: Transnational Diplomacy and Global Security/Economics of International Policy Making/International Bargaining and Decision Theory/Political Economy of Global Space and Environment/By Reason or By Force.

SELECTED FACULTY

Hayward Alker: Core theory and methods, conflict forecasting, world order and disorder.

Jonathan Aronson: International political economy, multilateral trade and trade regulation.

Laurie Brand: International relations of the Middle East, political economy of development with a specific focus on North-South relations and economic security.

Ann Tickner: Feminist perspectives on international relations theory with a particular focus on ways of reconceptualizing security.

Trinity College
International Studies Program
300 Summit Street
Hartford, CT 06106-3100
Phone: 860-297-2471
Fax: 860-297-5358

Web site: *www.trincoll.edu/depts/ints*
Degree: B.A.

The major in international studies at Trinity College offers concentrations in five areas of the world: Africa, Asia, Russia, the
Middle East, and Latin America and the Caribbean. A sixth concentration in comparative development studies allows students to
compare any two of these areas. All concentrations in international studies explore cultures through a range of disciplines,
including anthropology, sociology, economics, history, religion,
literature, political science, and the arts. Since entry to any culture
is gained through its language, a minimum of two years' relevant
language study is required. Students pursuing the international
studies major are strongly encouraged to include in their program
a period of off-campus study in an area of the world directly
linked to their research.

COURSE HIGHLIGHTS: Globalization, Rivalry, and Coordination/
World Population and Demography/Empire and Nationalism/
Gandhi, King, and Nonviolence/Religion and Culture Change/
Immigrants and Refugees/Theories of Revolution.

SELECTED FACULTY
Michael Niemann: Southern African politics and history.
Vijay Prashad: South Asian history; issues of racism, poverty,
oppression, and nonviolence.
Leslie Desmangles: Religion, cults, and sects in the Caribbean;
religion and cultural change; Caribbean pre-Columbian history.
Brigitte Schulz: Development, decolonization, the Cold War.

Tufts University
Program in International Relations
Cabot Intercultural Center, Room 605
Medford, MA 02155
Phone: 617-627-2776
Fax: 617-627-3083

Email: *omar.roca@tufts.edu*
Web site: *ase.tufts.edu/ir/*
Degree: B.A.

Established in 1977, Tufts University's undergraduate program in international relations (IR) draws on the strengths of sixteen departments and six related programs in both the social sciences and the humanities. Nearly 40 percent of Tufts IR majors pursue a double major, with languages and economics the leading affiliated concentrations. In addition to satisfying core and foreign language requirements, students choose coursework in one of five thematic clusters: foreign policy analysis; regional and comparative analysis; global conflict, cooperation, and justice; international economic and environmental affairs; and nationalism, culture, and identity. An independent study option is available, and two-thirds of majors pursue overseas study opportunities.

COURSE HIGHLIGHTS: Foundation of Liberal Societies/
World Religions and Economic Justice/Gender, Kinship, and
Person/East-West Perspectives on Fascism/The Nuclear Age: Its
History and Physics/Women and Law in the Middle East.

SELECTED FACULTY

Sugata Bose: Agrarian change in South Asia, development and distributive challenges in the age of globalism, nationalism and identity, comparative political economy.

Greg Carleton: Russia and the former USSR; Eastern Europe; issues of dissidence, persecution, and conflict in an intercultural context.

David Guss: Issues of globalization and transnationalization as they reflect on native and mestizo populations throughout Latin America.

Jeanne Penvenne: History of southern Africa; 20th-century social, cultural, labor and economic history; comparative women's history.

LABOR STUDIES

Cornell University
School of Industrial and Labor Relations
Ives Hall
Ithaca, NY 14853
Phone: 607-255-1812
Web site: *www.ilr.cornell.edu*
Degrees: B.S., M.S., Ph.D.

Founded in the 1940s, the School of Industrial and Labor Relations (ILR) is one of three statutory, or partially state-funded, academic schools at Cornell University. Cornell offers Bachelor of Science, Master of Science, and Doctor of Philosophy degrees in industrial and labor relations. The ILR defines itself as devoted to the study of workplace issues rather than strictly labor issues, so potential students should be aware that a certain proportion of the curriculum carries a business or management emphasis. Nonetheless, the labor-oriented faculty and coursework are regarded as among the strongest in the country.

Undergraduates choose one of the six departments of the ILR in which to concentrate their studies. These fields also serve as major and minor subject areas for students in the graduate division: collective bargaining, labor law, and labor history; human resource studies; international and comparative labor relations; labor economics; organizational behavior; and social statistics.

COURSE HIGHLIGHTS: Recent History of American Workers/ Global Industrial Relations/Labor Law and International Labor Rights/Labor Movements in Latin America/Building a Social Europe/Strangers and Citizens: Immigration and Labor in US History/Revitalizing the Labor Movement: A Comparative Perspective.

SELECTED FACULTY

Kate Bronfenbrenner: Organizing strategies, collective bargaining, contract administration.

Lance Compa: International labor law, international labor rights, social dimensions of international trade and investment.

Richard Hurd: US contemporary union movement, union organizing, union political action, organizational change in unions.

Lowell Turner: Comparative labor movements and labor revitalization, comparative political economy, labor and politics in unified Germany, European economic integration and industrial relations, industrial relations reform.

University of Massachusetts, Amherst

Labor Relations and Research Center
125 Draper Hall, Box 32020
Amherst, MA 01003-2020
Phone: 413-545-2884
Fax: 413-545-0110
Email: *info@lrrc.umass.edu*
Web site: *www.umass.edu/lrrc/*
Degree: M.S.

The Labor Relations and Research Center (LRRC) at the University of Massachusetts, Amherst offers a residential Master of Science in labor studies, a multidisciplinary program that combines coursework, an internship, and hands-on union experience. The LRRC's focus on globalization, labor and communities, and strategic corporate research equip graduates to work in the labor movement and other organizations advocating for workers' rights. Coursework toward the master's degree provides not only the skills necessary to work in and with the labor movement—expertise in organizing, collective bargaining, and union leadership—but also an opportunity to examine the larger theoretical and strategic issues confronting workers and their unions in the new millennium.

In 1995, the Center began offering an M.S. in labor studies in a limited-residency format for trade union officers, staff, and activists through an innovative program in cooperation with the George Meany Center for Labor Studies in Maryland. Trade unionists attend ten-day residencies in summer and winter and can complete their master's degree over a three-year period. The Union Leadership and Administration (ULA) program has quickly gained a national reputation and currently has more than one hundred trade unionists enrolled from across the US and Canada.

As part of a statewide extension program, the LRRC also offers noncredit training and education to unions and central labor bodies locally, statewide, and regionally. The Center's faculty and staff conduct research on labor issues, much of it funded by the labor movement.

COURSE HIGHLIGHTS: Corporate Research/Comparative Labor Movements/Labor in a Global Economy/Race and Ethnicity in the Labor Movement/Work Reorganization/Labor Research Methods/Collective Bargaining and Contract Administration.

SELECTED FACULTY

Tom Juravich: Union organizing, contract campaigns, union responses to employee involvement, work and the labor process, labor history and culture.
Frank Borgers: Economic globalization.
Stephanie Luce: Living wage movement.
Eve Weinbaum: Community response to plant closings, organizing, labor and politics.

Rutgers University
Department of Labor Studies and Employment Relations
50 Labor Center Way
New Brunswick, NJ 08903
Phone: 732-932-8559
Fax: 732-932-8677

Email: *mlirs@rci.rutgers.edu*
Web site: *www.rci.rutgers.edu/~smlr/*
Degrees: B.A., M.L.E.R., Ph.D.

The Department of Labor Studies and Employment Relations at Rutgers is part of the School of Management and Labor Relations, which offers a Ph.D. in industrial relations and human resources. The Master of Labor and Employment Relations (MLER) combines professional training with intellectual exploration to produce graduates who are thoughtful professionals, informed leaders, and/or researchers grounded in contemporary reality. Graduates go on to work in the public policy arena and public sector management and for labor organizations and corporations. The program is also appropriate for persons already working in human resources or labor relations who wish to examine contemporary problems and their solutions. Faculty and students are currently exploring globalization, the relation of work and family, contingent employment, new forms of work organization and compensation, workplace justice, privatization of public services, and new directions in collective bargaining. Courses are scheduled at times convenient for working adults and students may complete the program on either a full-time or part-time basis.

The Bachelor of Arts degree in labor studies and employment relations is embedded in the broader undergraduate curriculum of Rutgers' four liberal arts colleges: Rutgers College, Douglass College, Livingston College, and University College (the University's part-time, adult division). In order to major in this multidisciplinary course of study, students must take 36 credits of labor studies and employment relations courses as part of the total 120 credits required to graduate from Rutgers.

COURSE HIGHLIGHTS: Labor and Corporate Restructuring/ Globalization and the Future of Employment/Comparative Social and Labor Legislation/Employment Systems in Transitional Economies/Working Women in American Society.

SELECTED FACULTY

David Bensman: American labor history, education reform, impact of global economic integration on working people.
Dorothy Sue Cobble: Women and unions, gender and work, recent labor history.
Wells Keddie: Unions as institutions (especially in higher education), conflict resolution, public sector collective bargaining, theories of the labor movement.
Ryan Smith: Workplace stratification and racial attitudes in the US.

Also recommended

University of California, Los Angeles
Center for Labor Research and Education
School of Public Policy and Social Research
6350B Public Policy Building
Los Angeles, CA 90095-1478
Phone: 310-794-5981 or 794-5983
Fax: 310-794-6410
Email: *jamonroe@ucla.edu*
Web site: *labor.sppsr.ucla.edu*

The Labor Center at the University of California at Los Angeles administers an undergraduate specialization in labor and workplace studies. The specialization, essentially a minor, consists of six upper-division courses from a pre-selected group: three electives, two required, and one seminar in which the student works closely with a chosen faculty member. The Center acts as an important link between the academic community and the local labor movement.

George Meany Center for Labor Studies
National Labor College
10000 New Hampshire Avenue

Silver Spring, MD 20903
Phone: 301-431-6400 or 800-462-4237
Email: *nroy@georgemeany.org*
Web site: *www.georgemeany.org*

The National Labor College of the George Meany Center for Labor Studies has developed a unique program to satisfy the educational needs of trade union officers and staff members who cannot be served by traditional educational institutions and conventional educational mechanisms. The program is a flexible, largely external program that enables students to pursue a Bachelor of Arts degree while continuing their trade union work. It recognizes the educational value of the union experience that active officers and staff gain over the years, and credit is awarded for the learning that this experience has generated.

Wayne State University
College of Urban, Labor, and Metropolitan Affairs
656 West Kirby
Detroit, MI 48202
Phone: 313-577-5071
Web site: *www.culma.wayne.edu*

Wayne State University established the College of Urban, Labor, and Metropolitan Affairs (CULMA) in 1985 to coordinate and strengthen programming to advance the university's urban mission. CULMA has a special commitment to address the social, economic and political issues facing urban areas today and serves as the university's center for research, teaching, public service, and policy analysis in urban affairs and workplace issues. Wayne State is also home to the Walter P. Reuther Library, an outstanding archive of the American labor movement, and its history department contains several scholars with interests in labor history.

Youngstown State University
Center for Working Class Studies
John Russo, Co-director
Youngstown, OH 44555
Phone: 330-742-2976
Fax: 330-742-4622
Email: *jrusso@cc.ysu.edu*
Web site: *www.as.ysu.edu/~cwcs*

Started in 1996, the Center for Working Class Studies (CWCS) is an interdisciplinary research and teaching center at Youngstown State University (YSU) devoted to the study of working class life and culture. The Center develops courses in working class studies, organizes a biennial conference, publishes a newsletter, provides space for visiting scholars, and sponsors an annual speaker series. It houses a library and maintains a bibliography on working class studies to help promote scholarship in the field. At the undergraduate level, working class studies is an area of emphasis in the American Studies Program at Youngstown State University. Beginning in 2001, it will be possible to get a graduate certificate in the field.

LAW

American University
Washington College of Law
4801 Massachusetts Avenue, NW
Washington, DC 20016
Phone: 202-274-4000
Email: *wcladmit@wcl.american.edu*
Web site: *www.wcl.american.edu/*
Degrees: J.D., LL.M.

The Washington College of Law (WCL) at American University prides itself on its teaching, scholarship, and meaningful service to the legal profession and the world community. In its curriculum, pedagogy, and programs, WCL promotes intellectual pluralism, mutual respect, inculcation of the highest standards of legal professionalism, and the conscious interaction of theory, doctrine, and practice in the education of students. The degree of Juris Doctor is conferred upon students who satisfactorily complete 86 semester hours. This includes all required courses, with a quality point index of 2.0 ("C") or better; who are in residence for at least three full academic years or the equivalent; and who are recommended for the degree by the faculty. Residence requirements are met normally in six semesters (three academic years) of full-time study or in eight semesters (four academic years) of part-time study plus two summer sessions.

WCL offers clinical programs in civil practice, criminal justice, community and economic development law, international human rights law, and domestic violence/women and the law. It also grants Master of Law (LL.M.) degrees in international legal studies and law and government.

COURSE HIGHLIGHTS: International Environmental Law/ Antitrust Law/Seminar: Post-Conviction Remedies/Global Corruption/New Theories of Employment Discrimination/ Appellate Advocacy/International Humanitarian Law/Unfair Trade and Consumer Protection.

SELECTED FACULTY

Susan Bennett: Clinical education, community economic development, public interest law.

Mark Hager: Torts, labor and employment law, legal theory, legal history, international worker rights law, constitutional law.

Diane Orentlicher: International law, international organizations, human rights, ethnic identity.

Nancy Polikoff: Clinical education, family law, civil procedure.

Jamin Raskin: Constitutional law, criminal law and procedure, local government law.

University of California, Berkeley
School of Law
Boalt Hall
Berkeley, CA 94720-7200
Phone: 510-642-1741
Fax: 510-643-6171
Email: *admissions@law.berkeley.edu*
Web site: *www.law.berkeley.edu*
Degrees: J.D., LL.M., J.S.D. Ph.D.

The University of California, Berkeley School of Law (familiarly known as Boalt Hall) grants the J.D., LL.M., and J.S.D. degrees, as well as a Ph.D. in jurisprudence and social policy. At the J.D. level, the school offers specialized curricular programs in comparative legal studies, international legal studies, law and economics, law and technology, environmental law, and social justice/public interest. Boalt boasts a large and multifaceted clinical program, including a student-run community law center and clinics in international human rights, child advocacy, and federal practice.

Eleven concurrent degree programs are available through Boalt in cooperation with other departments at Berkeley. In addition, the school is home to numerous centers and institutes conducting research on a broad range of legal issues.

COURSE HIGHLIGHTS: Biodiversity and the Law/Visions of Justice and Accountability/International Law and Politics Workshop/Advanced Criminal Procedure: Prosecution Perspectives/Sexual Orientation and the Law/Law and Social Justice.

SELECTED FACULTY
John P. Dwyer: Environmental law.
Angela Harris: Feminist legal theory and critical race theory.

Rachel Moran: Chicano/Latino law and policy.
Robert Post: First Amendment theory and constitutional
jurisprudence.
Marjorie Shultz: Health care law, gender issues.

University of California, Davis
School of Law Admission Office
400 Mark Hall Drive
Davis, CA 95616-5201
Phone: 530-752-6477
Email: *lawadmissions@ucdavis.edu*
Web site: *kinghall.ucdavis.edu*
Degrees: J.D., LL.M.

The Law School of the University of California at Davis offers a comprehensive three-year curriculum leading to the J.D. degree, as well
as a combined degree program and a LL.M. Program. The three-
year curriculum is designed for full-time students only; no part-
time or evening program is offered. The coursework of the first year
is prescribed and provides the essential framework for subsequent
legal study. The work of the second and third years is elective, except
for a required course in legal ethics and a legal writing requirement.
Law students may receive credit for certain courses taken in other
departments of the University and for courses satisfactorily
completed in summer sessions at other accredited law schools.

The Law School has developed emphasis areas in environmental,
international, immigration, and public interest law. It offers academic credit in a variety of programs, including clinicals, public
interest, *pro bono*, moot court, trial practice and academic journals.
Clinical program fields include civil rights, immigration law, criminal justice, prison law, family protection, and environmental law.

COURSE HIGHLIGHTS: Environmental Justice Law Seminar/
Civil Rights Appeals Practicum/White Collar Crime/Public
Sector Labor Law Seminar/Housing and Community Develop-
ment Law/Use of Force/Latinos and Latinas and the Law.

SELECTED FACULTY

Diane Marie Amann: International criminal law, criminal law and procedure, evidence, constitutional law, international human rights law.

Bill Ong Hing: Clinical programs, ethnic studies, immigration policy, race relations.

James F. Smith: Human rights, international trade, mediation, cross-cultural communication, comparative constitutional law: United States, Latin America, Asia.

Martha West: Employment law.

Tobias Wolff: Free speech and the First Amendment; constitutional law; sex, sexuality, and the law; civil procedure and the federal courts; class actions; conflict of laws.

City University of New York

School of Law
65-21 Main Street
Flushing, NY 11367-1300
Phone: 718-340-4200
Email: *admissions@mail.law.cuny.edu*
Web site: *www.law.cuny.edu*
Degree: J.D.

Opened in 1983, CUNY School of Law is the only law school that, from its inception, has defined its mission as training law students for public service. The CUNY Law School faculty has developed a curriculum that integrates lawyering skills, practical experience, and professional responsibility with doctrinal study at every level. As a result, the Law School is a national leader in progressive legal education with the highest rate in the nation of placement of graduates in public interest and public service careers.

The Law School's lawyering program spans all three years of law school and designed to prepare each student for the practice of law. Beginning in the first year, students are introduced to lawyering skills and perspectives as part of the required curriculum. In the second year, students choose from a range of lawyering seminars that strengthen skills and knowledge to use in several different public interest areas. Finally, in their third year, students select from the Law School's highly regarded clinical program. Law clinics may include immigrant and refugee rights, elder law, international women's human rights, mediation, and indigent criminal defense, among others.

COURSE HIGHLIGHTS: Feminist Jurisprudence/Critical Race Theory/Poverty Law in the United States/Civil Disobedience and Law/Juvenile Rights/Evidence and Lawyering in the Public Interest/Law and Family Relations/Torts and Criminal Law.

SELECTED FACULTY

Paula Berg: Health care law.

Frank Deale: Employment discrimination, international labor rights.

Victor Goode: Affirmative action, housing, civil rights issues.

Dinesh Khosla: International law, contracts, civil disobedience, comparative law, law and aging, human rights, economic and social development.

Maivân Clech Lâm: Indigenous rights in international and United States constitutional law.

New York University School of Law

40 Washington Square South
Vanderbilt Hall
New York, NY 10012
Phone: 212-998-6100
Fax: 212-995-3156
Email: *law.jdadmissions@nyu.edu*
Web site: *www.law.nyu.edu*
Degrees: J.D., LL.M., LL.M. C.J., J.S.D.

The New York University School of Law offers rigorous programs at both the J.D. and graduate levels. The first year curriculum consists of courses on basic legal subjects—property, contracts, torts, criminal law, and civil procedure—along with a program in lawyering and a lecture series offering a diversity of legal perspectives. During the second and third years, students are free to shape a course of study that matches their interests, subject only to a writing requirement and to required courses in constitutional law and professional responsibility.

NYU Law's extensive array of institutes, centers, colloquia, and clinics complements classroom learning at all levels. Clinical programs are available in public policy advocacy, capital defense, civil legal services, civil rights, family defense, and juvenile rights, among other topics. The Public Interest Law Center (PILC), created in 1992, administers most of the Law School's public interest programs, including symposia, a *pro bono* project database, and scholarships and loan repayment assistance for public interest law students.

COURSE HIGHLIGHTS: Law's Authority: Democracy, Revolutions, and Coups/Global Public Service Lawyering: Theory and Practice/Indigenous Peoples in International Law/Intellectual Property, Traditional Communities, and Developing Countries/ Theory and Practice of Incarceration.

SELECTED FACULTY

Paula Galowitz: Poverty law, housing, immigration, public benefits, access to justice.
Randy Hertz: Capital defense, juvenile rights, lawyering theory.
Benedict Kingsbury: International institutions, theory of international law.
Sylvia Law: Women, health, poverty, constitutional law.
Gerald López: Race, immigration, poverty, economic development, civil rights litigation.

Northeastern University School of Law
400 Huntington Avenue
Boston, MA 02115

Phone: 617-373-5149
Fax: 617-373-8793
Email: *lawadmissions@nunet.neu.edu*
Web site: *www.slaw.neu.edu*
Degree: J.D.

Northeastern University's approach to training law students for a career in the legal profession is known as Cooperative Legal Education. Under this program, students complete a traditional first year of academic study and then, for the remaining two years, alternate every three months between working full time as legal interns and attending classes on a full-time basis. The successful completion of four cooperative work quarters is a graduation requirement for all Northeastern law students. Approximately 190 students are employed each quarter in a variety of legal practices, including private firms (all sizes), legal services, public defender associations, judicial clerkships (state and federal, trial and appellate), government agencies, corporate legal departments, unions and special interest advocacy organizations.

The School is home to a number of law clinics oriented toward social justice, among them programs in criminal appeals, domestic violence, poverty law and practice, and prisoners' rights. All students must fulfill a public interest requirement prior to graduation. The requirement may be fulfilled in one of several ways, including completion of a public interest co-op, completion of any of the law school's clinical courses, performance of at least 30 hours of uncompensated legal work in a public interest setting or with a private firm on a *pro bono* project, or a public interest independent study.

COURSE HIGHLIGHTS: Seminar: Bioethics and the Law/
Self-Determination, Human Rights, and the Law of War/Race,
Gender, Juries, and Justice/Mediation-in-the-Public-Interest
Seminar/Environmental Decision-Making/Battered Women
and the Law.

SELECTED FACULTY

Clare Dalton: Domestic violence, torts, contracts, modern legal theory and bioethics.

Daniel Givelber: Criminal law, criminal procedure and torts, death penalty litigation.

James Rowan: Community legal education, economic development and grassroots organizing.

Lucy A. Williams: Poverty and social welfare law.

Margaret Y. K. Woo: Chinese legal reform, human rights, gender equality.

PEACE STUDIES

University of California, Berkeley
Peace and Conflict Studies
101 Stephens Hall
Berkeley, CA 94720
Phone: 510-642-4466
Fax: 510-642-9850
Email: *iastp@uclink.berkeley.edu*
Web site: *www.ias.berkeley.edu/iastp/pacs/pacs.html*
Degree: B.A.

The Peace and Conflict Studies major at the University of California, Berkeley prepares students to understand the dynamics of peace and conflict and to contribute to the creation of more just and peaceable conditions in the world. Courses focus on the understanding of conflict, the history of peace efforts, conflict resolution, human rights, and world order. All students complete core and survey courses, select an area of concentration, demonstrate foreign language competency, and fulfill an internship requirement.

COURSE HIGHLIGHTS: Peace Theories/Nonviolence Today/ Multi-Cultural Conflict Resolution/Global Change and World Order/Human Rights and American Cultures/Special Topics in Regional Conflict/War, Culture, and Society.

SELECTED FACULTY

Claudia Carr: Alternative rural development policies.
Diane Clemens: American history since 1607, diplomatic history.
Charles Henry: African American politics and public policy.
David Leonard: Public administration and the politics of development, focusing on Africa.
Beth Simmons: International relations, political economy, and law.

Earlham College

Peace and Global Studies Program
Box 105
Richmond, IN 47374
Phone: 765-983-1305 or 765-983-1502
Email: *dortham@earlham.edu*
Web site: *www.earlham.edu/~pags/*
Degree: B.A.

Earlham College's Peace and Global Studies (PAGS) program has gained a national and international reputation in its twenty years of existence. This recognition emerges from Earlham's solid commitment to peace education as it derives from the Quaker identity of the institution, from the presence of a number of faculty with national recognition in the field of peace research, and from the unusual mixture of opportunities provided at the undergraduate and graduate levels through religious studies at the Earlham School of Religion. The program has sought to implement its goals by infusing peace studies into the entire curriculum. A four-course introductory sequence, required of all PAGS majors, satisfies the general education requirements at the college as well as providing alternative introductory courses to the disciplines of philosophy, politics, and economics. More than 80 percent of Earlham graduates have taken at least one of these courses. Students who wish to major in peace and global studies or to design a joint major with another field should submit their proposed major to the PAGS committee. An internship and senior seminar are required.

COURSE HIGHLIGHTS: Theory and Practice of Nonviolence/ Politics of Global Problems/Ethics and World Food Policy/ Conflict Resolution/Theories of International Relations/Issues Before the United Nations/Totalitarianism and Transformation.

SELECTED FACULTY

Jonathan Diskin: Political economy, Marxism.

Barbara Welling Hall: Impact of information technology on change in international relations, the politics of transformation in the former Soviet Union.

Caroline Higgins: Latin American studies; peace, pedagogy, and empowerment.

Howard Richards: Philosophical and theological views on peace and justice.

George Mason University
Institute for Conflict Analysis and Resolution
Fairfax, VA 22030-4444
Phone: 703-993-1300
Fax: 703-993-1302
Email: *icarinfo@osf1.gmu.edu*
Web site: *www.gmu.edu/departments/icar/*
Degrees: M.S., Ph.D.

The Institute for Conflict Analysis and Resolution at George Mason University offers the Ph.D. and M.S. degrees in conflict analysis and resolution. Major research interests include the analysis of deep-rooted conflicts and their resolution; exploration of conditions attracting parties to the negotiation table; role of third parties in dispute resolution; and the testing of a variety of conflict intervention methods in community, national, and international settings. In addition to its degree programs, the Institute sponsors research and publications, a clinical and consultancy program, and public outreach.

The Master of Science two-year program integrates theory and conflict resolution processes such as negotiation, mediation, third-party consultation, and analytical problem solving. Students study the theory, methods, and ethical perspectives of the field and apply this knowledge both in laboratory-simulation and workshop courses, and in field internships. The latter are contracted with agencies in the Washington, DC area and elsewhere, including abroad. The doctoral program, the first of its kind in the United States, provides advanced study for students in the fields of conflict and conflict resolution. Students are prepared to qualify as researchers, theoreticians, and teachers in higher education; and as policy administrators, analysts, and consultants in both public and private sectors.

COURSE HIGHLIGHTS: Global Context of Conflict/Conflict in Development/Theories of Social Harmony/Conflict Termination: Dynamics of the Peace Process/Party Roles, Resources, and Ethics in Conflict Resolution/Peace Keeping/Peace Building/ Reconciliation.

SELECTED FACULTY

Kevin Avruch: Cultural and ethnic conflict, peacemaking, Middle East regional issues.
Ho Won Jeong: Theory and dynamics of conflict resolution, ethnic and international conflict, global political economy.
Michelle Lebaron: Gender and conflict, environmental and public policy, family conflict, law and dispute resolution.
Richard Rubenstein: Political violence, media and conflict, religious conflict.

University of Notre Dame
Joan B. Kroc Institute for International Peace Studies
100 Hesburgh Center for International Studies

PO Box 639
Notre Dame, IN 46556-0639
Phone: 219-631-6970
Fax: 219-631-6973
Email: *krocinst@nd.edu*
Web site: *www.nd.edu/~krocinst/*
Degree: M.A.

The Joan B. Kroc Institute for International Peace Studies at the University of Notre Dame conducts educational, research, and outreach programs on international peace. The Institute's programs emphasize international norms and institutions; religious, philosophical, and cultural dimensions of peace; conflict transformation; and social, economic, and environmental justice.

The Kroc Institute offers a unique and challenging multidisciplinary program of graduate study leading to the Master of Arts degree in peace studies. The eleven-month program attracts outstanding students from around the world and equips them with theoretical understanding and practical skills. Although a Ph.D. degree is not offered, students enrolled in a doctoral degree program in a traditional department such as government and international studies, economics, sociology, or theology may elect to take selected coursework in peace and world order studies as a sub-field or a complement to their major field, or may pursue dissertation research under the guidance of the faculty in the Institute. The concentration in peace studies is a multidisciplinary program available to all Notre Dame undergraduates who want to complement their major field with courses focused on issues of peace, violence, justice, and human rights.

COURSE HIGHLIGHTS: Origins of Violence–Cultures of Peace/ War, Human Rights, and Peacebuilding/Democratic Theory and Multiculturalism/Political Economy of Post-Industrial Societies/ Comparative Religious Fundamentalism/Conflict Transformation.

SELECTED FACULTY

Denis A. Goulet: Development ethics and indicators, comparative development strategies, environmental economics.
Gil Loescher: International refugee policy.
Carolyn Nordstrom: Political anthropology of peace and conflict, medical anthropology, gender issues, culture theory, Africa and Asia.
Raimo Väyrynen: Theory of international relations, international security and disarmament, international political economy, peace and conflict studies.

San Diego State University

Institute for International Security and Conflict Resolution
5500 Campanile Drive
San Diego, CA 92182
Phone: 619-594-2778
Fax: 619-594-7302
Email: *djohns@mail.sdsu.edu*
Web site: *www-rohan.sdsu.edu/dept/iiscor/*
Degree: B.A.

San Diego State University offers an undergraduate major in international security and conflict resolution. Completion of two sets of requirements provides breadth and depth for the major. The first set includes interdisciplinary courses addressing international security and conflict resolution; the second set is drawn from a specialization in one of the following: global systems; cooperation, conflict, and conflict resolution; or environment and security. Students must either complete a supervised internship or write a thesis. Competency in a foreign language is required, and overseas study is highly recommended.

The Institute for International Security and Conflict Resolution (IISCOR) at San Diego State encourages and facilitates teaching and research in the multidisciplinary area of international security and conflict resolution. IISCOR addresses such topics as nuclear armaments, international and infra-national conflict, sociopolitical violence, and global environmental issues as they relate to security.

COURSE HIGHLIGHTS: International Security in the Nuclear Age/Our Global Future: Values for Survival/Protests, Reforms, and Revolutions/Politics of the Environment/World Cities: Comparative Approaches to Urbanization/History of Corporations in the Modern World.

SELECTED FACULTY

Ann Cottrell: Field research methods, cross-cultural sociology, comparative sociology, global systems, social change.
Paul Ganster: Environmental issues of the US-Mexican border region.
James Gerber: International economic relations, US economic history, economies of Latin America in the post-World War II era.
David Johns: International and comparative politics, with emphasis on the Middle East.

Tufts University
Peace and Justice Studies Program
109 Eaton Hall
Medford, MA 02155
Phone: 617-627-2261
Fax: 617-627-3032
Email: *dale.bryan@tufts.edu*
Web site: *ase.tufts.edu/pjs/*
Degree: B.A.

The Peace and Justice Studies program (PJS) at Tufts University brings intellectual and experiential inquiry to the fundamental interrelationship of peace and justice. Four overlapping areas are emphasized: first, study of the causes of war, the techniques of war prevention, and the conditions and structures of a just peace;

second, the origins, strategies, and visions of social movements seeking social justice and ecological sustainability; third, the theory and practice of conflict resolution along a continuum from individual disputes to international diplomacy; and fourth, the study of peace culture, particularly the contributions from education and literature in developing the traditions of nonviolence and ethical social behavior. The program encourages both experiential education, primarily through internship placements and community-service learning, and discussion of appropriate pedagogy designed to promote the participation of students in their own education. Administering PJS is an executive board composed of faculty, students, and staff.

To fulfill the requirements for the major, students must complete ten courses: an introductory course, an internship, an integrative seminar, three electives on a particular theme to be chosen in consultation with the student's adviser, and four intermediate courses, one from each of the following groupings: war and peace, social movements, conflict resolution, and peace cultures. A senior project is also required.

COURSE HIGHLIGHTS: Nonprofit Organizations in Civic Action and Public Policy/Anthropology of War and Peacemaking/ Transnational Social Movements/Religion and International Relations/Interpersonal Conflict and Negotiation/Race in America.

SELECTED FACULTY

Dale Bryan: Social movements and nonviolence.
Richard Eichenberg: Public opinion, national security, European integration.
Gerald Gill: African American and recent US history, US South since 1865.
Paul Joseph: Sociology of war and peace, political sociology.

POLITICAL SCIENCE

Brooklyn College
Department of Political Science
City University of New York
2900 Bedford Avenue
Brooklyn, NY 11210
Phone: 718-951-5306
Fax: 718-951-4833
Web site: *academic.brooklyn.cuny.edu/polisci/*
Degrees: B.A., M.A.

Brooklyn College of the City University of New York offers the
B.A. and M.A. in political science. In addition to core and distribution courses, undergraduates must take a total of seven elective
courses chosen from the following four departmental sub-fields:
American politics and urban politics, international politics, comparative politics, and political theory and methodology. At least
one course must be chosen from each field.

Students in the M.A. program have the option of a comprehensive examination or a thesis to complete the requirements for
the degree. A minimum of nine credits in one sub-field and three
in each of the other three areas is required. Students must demonstrate proficiency in a language other than their native language by
passing a foreign language test approved by the department. A
Doctor of Jurisprudence–Master of Arts joint degree program is
available in cooperation with the Brooklyn Law School.

COURSE HIGHLIGHTS: Postindustrial Politics and the
State/Changing Concepts and Practices in International
Cooperation/Politics and Public Opinion Formation/
Regionalism in World Politics/Interest Groups in American
Society/Communist Political Systems

SELECTED FACULTY

Sally Bermanzohn: Race and gender in American politics, social welfare policy, New York City government.

Vincent Fuccillo: American political thought, Western European politics.

Immanuel Ness: Labor and labor politics, political parties, urban politics.

Mark Ungar: Human rights, international law, policing, judicial reform and democracy in Latin America.

Cornell University
Department of Government
McGraw Hall
Ithaca, NY 14853-4601
Phone: 607-255-3549
Fax: 607-255-4530
Email: *cu_govt@cornell.edu*
Web site: *falcon.arts.cornell.edu/govt/*
Degrees: B.A., M.A., Ph.D.

Cornell University's Department of Government is devoted to the study of political power and the interaction of citizens and governments. The department offers special opportunities within its undergraduate major, including a concentration in international relations, a study abroad program, an independent study option, and the Cornell-in-Washington program. Students in the honors program take an organized seminar in their senior year, as well as work with an individual faculty member on their senior thesis.

The graduate program in government is designed to prepare students for academic and research careers as political scientists competent in the theory, methods, and substance of the discipline. Students who are admitted to the program are expected to get a Ph.D. degree. Only under exceptional circumstances are students admitted as M.A. candidates, but students who choose to leave the program or who fail to fulfill the requirements for admission to Ph.D. candidacy may be granted a master's degree. Completion of the Ph.D. program normally requires two to three years of full-time coursework and research at Cornell, and two or more years of dissertation research and writing. Ph.D. students must demonstrate competence in either a foreign language or statistics, and do at least three major research papers prior to admission to candidacy.

COURSE HIGHLIGHTS: Plural Society Revisited/Social Movements, Collective Action, and Reform/The Quality of Democracy in Latin America/Sovereignty and International Politics/Public Opinion and Political Participation/Feminist Movements and the State.

SELECTED FACULTY

Mary Fainsod Katzenstein: Feminism, women's movements and state policies, Indian politics, gender and ethnicity.
Jonas G. Pontusson: Western Europe, political economy, comparative labor movements.
Judith Reppy: Peace studies, the military, science and technology.
Norman T. Uphoff: Third World and sustainable development, development administration, local institutions and participation, South Asia, public policy.

Illinois State University
Department of Political Science
306 Schroeder Hall
Normal, IL 61790-4600
Phone: 309-438-7638
Web site: *lilt.ilstu.edu/politicalscience/*
Degrees: B.A., B.S., M.A., M.S.

The political science program at Illinois State University provides undergraduates with the opportunity to study the operation of government and the manner in which individuals and interest groups can affect government policy. Courses cover topics such as the presidency, Congress, the courts, public opinion and elections, political parties, state and local governments, public administration, public policy, international relations, comparative governments, and political theory. Concentrations in public service or global studies are available, and the department offers undergraduate teaching and research assistantships.

The department's graduate program in political science promotes knowledge and skills in the areas of scholarship, teaching, and service in and about the political dimensions of social life. Courses and program options exist for students who are planning to pursue further graduate education as well as students who, for reasons of career enhancement or specialized training for employment, are seeking a master's degree as their ultimate goal. Concentrations in public service, global studies, and applied community development are available.

COURSE HIGHLIGHTS: US Politics and Culture after Vietnam/ Political Theories of Nonviolence/Politics, Budgets, and Taxes/ Politics of Federalism/Campaign Politics/Comparative Foreign Policy and Process/Global Issues.

SELECTED FACULTY

Robert Hunt: Non-Western politics, community development, global issues, comparative development theory.

Janie Leatherman: Conflict resolution, peace studies, international relations theory, international organizations, postcommunist transitions in Central and Eastern Europe.

Jamal Nassar: Methodology of comparative politics and international relations, the Middle East, development, global interdependence.

Carlos Parodi: US foreign policy and intervention, nationalism and globalization in Latin America.

Manfred Steger: Comparative political theory, political violence and its alternatives, social theory, Marxism and social democracy, politics and ethics.

Lehigh University
Department of Political Science
Maginnes Hall
9 West Packer Avenue
Bethlehem, PA 18015
Phone: 610-758-3340
Fax: 610-758-6554
Web site: *www.lehigh.edu/~ingov/homepage.html*
Degrees: B.A., M.A.

Lehigh University's undergraduate major in political science is designed to promote understanding of political ideas, institutions, and processes, and to develop skills in analyzing and evaluating political problems. Three core courses and six electives are required for the major. The department offers a community politics internship every semester that includes opportunities for internship placements in local government, private agencies, or law offices. Other experiential opportunities are available.

The M.A. program in political science prepares students for public service careers and/or further graduate study in political science, public policy, or law. The program is intended for the student with a liberal arts background who is interested in politics and the public policy arena. To complete the master's program, students must accumulate 30 credit hours (four core courses and a research methods class plus 15 additional credits, including at least one team-based community project). A comprehensive examination or thesis is also required. Particular emphasis is placed on close faculty-student interaction both in classes and hands-on projects with local or regional partners. The department is in the process of developing a graduate focus on advocacy and policy.

COURSE HIGHLIGHTS: Propaganda, Media Culture, and American Politics/Urban Politics/National Social Policy/US Foreign Policy in Latin America/The Citizen versus the Administrative State/Socialization and the Political System/ Green Polity.

SELECTED FACULTY

Richard K. Matthews: Political philosophy with a specialization in ideologies and early American political thought.

Edward Morgan: Government and propaganda, the media, US foreign policy.

Hannah Stewart-Gambino: Comparative politics, Third World politics, Latin America.

Albert Wurth: American public policy and political economy, with an emphasis on the environment and technology.

University of Minnesota

Department of Political Science
1414 Social Sciences Building
267 19th Avenue South
Minneapolis, MN 55455
Phone: 612-624-4144
Fax: 612-626-7599
Email: *office@polisci.umn.edu*
Web site: *www.polisci.umn.edu*
Degrees: B.A., M.A., Ph.D.

The University of Minnesota's Department of Political Science offers programs leading to the B.A., Ph.D., and professional or terminal M.A. Undergraduate students meet distribution requirements in the sub-fields of American government, comparative government, international relations, and political theory. All majors must complete a senior paper, and honors students attend a seminar and write a more substantial thesis. Individualized research, fieldwork, and internship opportunities are available, and political science students are eligible for several merit-based scholarship awards.

The Ph.D. program accepts applications from students completing or holding B.A. degrees as well as students with M.A. degrees. Full funding is provided for at least three years to all entering Ph.D. students. Doctoral candidates develop expertise in two of the sub-fields listed above with methodology as an additional choice. They also gain a wider understanding by taking social science and/or humanities courses in other departments and by taking political science courses in areas that are not in their fields of concentration. This breadth/depth combination has proved a major aspect of the program's appeal. The University's Faculty and T.A. Enrichment Program assists graduate students in the acquisition of teaching and other professional skills.

A master's degree program is offered to students who are interested in post-baccalaureate education in political science but not in college teaching or research at the Ph.D. level. Secondary school teachers, journalists, government employees, political professionals and others may wish to enroll in this program in order to cover the substance of broad areas of study in political science and related disciplines without the depth and extensive research emphasized in the Ph.D. program.

COURSE HIGHLIGHTS: Welfare State Theories and American Social Policy/International Hierarchy/International Relations of the Environment/Comparative Mass Political Behavior/Norms and Institutions in International Relations/Global Governance.

SELECTED FACULTY

Raymond Duvall: International political economy and international relations theory, especially with respect to international hierarchy and the institutions of global capitalism.
Colin Kahl: Civil and ethnic conflict, causes of war, demographic change in developing countries, global environmental politics, international relations theory.
August Nimtz: African politics, urban politics, social movements, political development and Marxism.
Richard Price: Morality and norms in world politics, international relations theory, technology and violence, international law.
Kathryn Sikkink: Latin American politics, human rights, transnational social movements and issue networks, Third World development.

New School University
Department of Political Science, Room 250
Graduate Faculty of Political and Social Science
65 Fifth Avenue
New York, NY 10003
Phone: 212-229-5747
Fax: 212-807-1669
Email: *gfadmit@newschool.edu*
Web site (university): *www.newschool.edu/gf/polsci/*

Eugene Lang College
65 West 11th Street
New York, NY 10011
Phone: 212-229-5665
Web site (college): *www.lang.edu*
Degrees: B.A., M.A., Ph.D., D.S.Sc.

The Department of Political Science at New School University (formerly known as the New School for Social Research) offers M.A., Ph.D., and Doctor of Social Science degrees. The graduate faculty emphasizes the theoretical dimension of political analysis and the historical roots of contemporary political forces and problems. The department's curriculum is organized into three tracks: political theory; growth and structure of the American polity; and state and society in global perspective. Students in the department are members of a community of scholars constituted by faculty and students from the graduate faculty as a whole. The Department of Political Science contributes actively to this community through classes, research projects and conferences on subjects of widely shared interest. Students also have an opportunity to participate in departmental affairs through the Union of Political Science Students.

Eugene Lang College, the undergraduate liberal arts college of New School University, also offers courses in political science. Students at the college are encouraged to draw upon the resources of the entire university in designing their programs of study. An accelerated B.A./M.A. degree is available.

COURSE HIGHLIGHTS: Liberal Theories of Democracy and Their Critics/Left Politics in the US Under Neoliberalism/Slavery and Freedom in Western Political Thought/Identity, Class, and Human Rights in a Global World/The Social Contract and Its Critics.

SELECTED FACULTY

Nancy Fraser: Globalization, social justice, multiculturalism, feminism.
James Miller: History of political thought, democratic theory, social movements and political culture, contemporary philosophy, cultural criticism, philosophy as a way of life.
Adamantia Pollis: Comparative politics, human rights, nationalism and ethnicity.
Adolph Reed: African American politics, urban and social policy.

York University
Department of Political Science
Ross Building S672
4700 Keele Street
Toronto, Ontario
CANADA M3J 1P3
Phone: 416-736-5265
Fax: 416-736-5686
Email (undergraduate admissions): *admenq@yorku.ca*
Email (graduate admissions): *gradinfo@yorku.ca*
Web site: *www.yorku.ca/polisci/*
Degrees: B.A., M.A., Ph.D.

The York University Political Science Department has a reputation for research excellence and is noted for its commitments to teaching, interdisciplinary studies, and political change. Its object is to expand critical awareness of political problems and to help overcome the barriers that separate politics from social life and the university from the community. The undergraduate program in Political Science offers the following fields of specialization: political theory, international relations, comparative world politics, Canadian government and politics, and empirical theory and methodology.

The M.A. generally takes a full calendar year to complete, with the summer term devoted to completing the research paper or thesis. The two options for the M.A. are either three full-year courses (or their equivalent in full- and half-year courses) plus the M.A. research paper, or two full courses plus an M.A. thesis. All M.A. students must enroll in the M.A. colloquium, a half-credit course graded on a pass/fail basis. The M.A. colloquium seeks to familiarize students with the range of scholarly work in which members of the political science faculty are engaged. York also offers a part-time M.A. program. The Ph.D. program generally requires at least four years of full-time study, with considerable variation depending on the nature of the candidate's dissertation research. Faculty regulations require the completion of all requirements no later than six years after enrollment.

York International *(international.yorku.ca)* provides information on visas, financial aid, and general orientation to students from outside Canada.

COURSE HIGHLIGHTS: Development and the Modern Corporation: Limits and Possibilities/The State, Restructuring, and the North American Economic Block/The Idea of Democracy/ Histories and Theories of Nationalism/Post-Fordism: Order and Disorder in the Global Economy/Canadian Federalism in Comparative Perspective.

SELECTED FACULTY

George Comninel: Revolutions, European political theory considered in a socio-historical context, comparative study of the development of state and society.
David Mutimer: Critical security studies; nonproliferation, arms

control and disarmament; theory and practice in contemporary
international security.
Leo Panitch: Socialism and democracy, working class politics,
state theory, corporatism, comparative political economy,
Canadian politics, British politics.
Patricia Stamp: African political economy, local government in
the Third World, gender relations in the Third World, feminist
and discourse theory.

PUBLIC HEALTH/NUTRITION

Boston University
School of Public Health
715 Albany Street
Talbot Street
Boston, MA 02118
Phone: 617-638-4640
Fax: 617-638-5299
Email: *bso@bu.edu*
Web site: *www.bumc.bu.edu/sph*
Degrees: M.P.H., M.Sc., D.Sc.

The School of Public Health (SPH) at Boston University offers
degree programs leading to the Master of Public Health (M.P.H.),
the Master of Science (M.Sc.) in epidemiology, and the Doctor of
Science (D.Sc.) in epidemiology and environmental health sciences.
A Doctor of Public Health (Dr.P.H.) degree program is expected
to begin in September 2001. The school's Department of
International Health offers a variety of intensive, short-term certificate programs for health professionals with an interest in
health care in developing countries.

To earn the Master of Public Health degree, students must satisfactorily complete 48 credits of coursework, including 16 credits of core courses, between 16 and 20 credits of concentration courses depending on concentration, and the remainder in electives. Students must satisfy the requirements of one (or more) of the following concentrations: environmental health; epidemiology and biostatistics; health law; health services; international health; maternal and child health; health behavior, health promotion, and disease prevention (in the Social and Behavioral Sciences Department). The Field Practice Program, under the direction of the Public Health Practice Office, allows students to gain valuable work experience in local, state, federal, and international organizations on a wide variety of projects. Working closely with a faculty preceptor, students are supervised by professionals in the field (including SPH alumni), and earn academic credit.

COURSE HIGHLIGHTS: Nutrition and Food Policy in the Developing World/Comparative Health Systems and Health Sector Reform/Consumer Advocacy and Organizing: Making Health Care Respond to the Needs of Underserved People/Urban Environmental Health.

SELECTED FACULTY

Hortensia Amaro: Ethnic and cultural differences in health behavior and health problems, development and evaluation of community-based prevention/intervention programs.

Michael Grodin: Medical and public health ethics, human experimentation, human genetics, survivors of torture and refugee trauma, health and human rights.

H. Kristian Heggenhougen: Medical anthropology, equity and health, human rights and health.

Lois McCloskey: Access to and quality of health care services for women and children in urban communities, reproductive health policy, community-based program evaluation.

Alan Sager: Equal access to effective acute and ambulatory care, hospital finance, survival of needed hospitals, affordable prescription drugs.

Cornell University
Division of Nutritional Sciences
309 Martha Van Rensselaer Hall
Cornell University
Ithaca, NY 14853
Phone: 607-255-4410
Email: *nutrition_gfr@cornell.edu*
Web site: *www.nutrition.cornell.edu*
Degrees: B.S., M.S., Ph.D., M.P.S. (Human Ecology)

The Division of Nutritional Sciences (DNS) at Cornell University was established in 1974 through a union of the Graduate School of Nutrition, an autonomous graduate school at Cornell University, and the Department of Food and Nutrition in the College of Human Ecology. It is the largest academic unit in the United States devoted to human nutrition. It is also one of the most diversified, with expertise in molecular and human nutrition, nutrition education, nutritional qualities of food, international nutrition, and food policy. At the graduate level, the school offers concentrations in animal nutrition, community nutrition, human nutrition, international nutrition, and nutritional biochemistry. Undergraduates enrolled in the College of Human Ecology may select a major in nutritional sciences or one in human biology, health, and society. Students enrolled in the College of Agriculture and Life Sciences may select a major in nutrition, food, and agriculture.

The Division is home to a number of formal and informal outreach programs. The Cornell Food and Nutrition Policy program, for example, plays important roles in the analysis of alternative policies and in framing the debate on the role of the state in promoting equitable growth.

COURSE HIGHLIGHTS: Nutrition Intervention in Communities: A Global Perspective/Topics in Maternal and Child Nutrition/ Community Nutrition Research Seminar/National and International Food Economics/Nutritional Problems of Developing Nations.

SELECTED FACULTY

Carol M. Devine: Nutrition interventions for culturally diverse audiences.
Edward Frongillo: Nutritional well-being of the disadvantaged in the US and developing countries, food insecurity, poor child growth, program evaluation, nutritional assessment.
Ardyth H. Gillespie: Nutrition communication, nutrition education, community nutrition.
Michael C. Latham: International nutrition and tropical public health.
David L. Pelletier: Nutrition policies and programs in the US and developing countries.

Emory University
Department of International Health
Rollins School of Public Health
1518 Clifton Road NE
Atlanta, GA 30322
Phone: 404-727-8720
Email: *admit@sph.emory.edu*
Web site: *www.sph.emory.edu*
Degrees: M.P.H., Ph.D.

The Department of International Health at Emory University offers a course of study leading to the Master of Public Health (M.P.H.) degree. Flexibility and personalized attention are hallmarks of the program. Only about half of the 42 credits required for a degree are core requirements of the school and the department. This allows students to select from among four areas of concentration: infectious diseases, public nutrition, population studies and reproductive health, and community health. Diversity in ethnic and national origin characterizes the student body. The department hosts eight to ten Humphrey Fellows each year; these are mid-career professionals from developing countries who are selected for their leadership potential. The department cosponsors the Ph.D. program in nutrition and health sciences with other units of Emory University and the US Centers for Disease Control and Prevention. M.P.H. graduates have successfully gained admission to the Ph.D. program.

The Emory Human Rights Certificate program is a student-initiated project that seeks to identify interdisciplinary solutions to human rights and social justice problems by bringing together public health students and faculty with peers in other graduate disciplines, such as law, medicine, nursing, business, theology, and arts and sciences. The program is inspired by the World Health Organization's definition of health as "a state of complete physical, mental, and social well-being, not merely the absence of disease or infirmity," as well as the realization that many public health problems are in fact rooted in conditions of social inequality. The curriculum includes a mandatory service-learning component, giving students the opportunity to link human rights theory to its real-world application.

COURSE HIGHLIGHTS: Public Health Impacts of War and Terrorism/Health, Culture, and Communities/International Health: Anthropological Perspectives/Global Elimination of Micronutrient Malnutrition/Global Perspectives in Parasitic Diseases.

SELECTED FACULTY

Jennifer Hirsch: Gender, sexuality, and reproductive health; migration; qualitative methods.
Reynaldo Martorell: Protein-energy malnutrition, functional consequences of malnutrition, design and evaluation of nutrition interventions, food and nutrition policy.

Deborah McFarland: Comparative health policy, health system finance and reform, equity and the poor.
Kathryn Yount: Gender and population, male fertility and contraceptive preferences, reproductive health in the Middle East.

Tufts University
School of Nutrition Science and Policy
126 Curtis Street
Medford, MA 02155
Phone: 617-627-3923
Fax: 617-627-3887
Email: *nutritionadmissions@tufts.edu*
Web site: *nutrition.tufts.edu/school/admissions/*
Degrees: M.S., Ph.D.

The School of Nutrition Science and Policy at Tufts University consists of eight separate degree-granting programs as well as a number of dual and combined degrees. The program in agriculture, food, and environment addresses growing interest in the interconnections among environmental, social, nutritional, and safety aspects of food production and supply. It offers M.S. and Ph.D. degrees, diverse community service and internship placements, and opportunities to participate in research on sustainable agriculture, local food systems, and consumer behavior related to food and the environment. The degree program combines Tufts University's strengths in nutrition, health sciences, environmental sciences, international development, and environmental policy. The Food Policy and Applied Nutrition (FPAN) program offers specializations in food policy and economics; nutrition interventions: design, operation, and management; and humanitarian assistance. FPAN provides not only the conceptual and analytical skills required by program managers and policy analysts, but also a solid foundation in applied statistical and research skills as well as in technical aspects of program planning, design, implementation, and evaluation.

The Master of Arts in humanitarian assistance is a one-year combined degree offered by the School of Nutrition Science and Policy and the Fletcher School of Law and Diplomacy at Tufts University. The program is geared toward mid-career professionals who have significant field experience in humanitarian assistance. Tufts University offers an academic setting where professionals can develop their knowledge and skills in the areas of nutrition; food policy; and economic, political, and social development as they relate to humanitarian assistance in famine, complex emergencies, and other disasters. Practitioners study, read about, reflect on, and write about humanitarian theories, programs, and policies.

COURSE HIGHLIGHTS: Political and Social Change in Developing Countries/Income, Food Prices, and Nutrition/Environment and Food Supply/Global Food Business/Daily Risks and Crisis Events: How People and Planners Cope with Vulnerability/Ethics of Humanitarianism and Development.

SELECTED FACULTY

Steven Block: Food and agricultural policy in developing countries, agricultural productivity, development economics, political economy.
Sue Lautze: Patterns of trade across conflict zones, emergency asset protection strategies, capacity building, strategic humanitarian response.
William Moomaw: Sustainable development, trade and environment, technology and policy implications for climate change, water and climate change, biodiversity.
Beatrice Rogers: Food policy and economics, intra-household resource allocation, consumer food price policy, food consumption effects of economic policies, food aid.

Tulane University
School of Public Health and Tropical Medicine
1440 Canal Street, Suite 2430
New Orleans, LA 70112-2824

Phone: 504-588-5387 or 800-676-5389
Fax: 504-584-1667
Email: *adminsph-l@tulane.edu*
Web site: *www.sph.tulane.edu*
Degrees: M.P.H., M.S.P.H., Master of health administration
(M.H.A.), Master of public health and tropical medicine (M.P.H.
& T.M.), Master of applied development and health (M.A.D.H.),
Master of medical management (M.M.M), Doctor of Public
Health (Dr.P.H.), Doctor of Science (Sc.D.)

Tulane University's School of Public Health and Tropical Medicine
offers academic graduate degree programs in biostatistics, epidemiology, environmental health (water quality management,
industrial hygiene, toxicology and risk assessment, and occupational health), health education/communication, health systems
management, hospital administration, international health and
development, maternal and child health, nutrition, parasitology,
population studies, and tropical medicine. The school has established priority emphasis areas of health and the environment,
health policy and management, international public health, tropical medicine, women's health, and public health practice.

The curriculum is designed to provide in-depth study in a
specific discipline in combination with a breadth of study of
public health principles. Each student selects a program of study
in one of the school's seven departments and must complete all
requirements for that program. In addition, students must satisfactorily complete a set of core courses in biostatistics, epidemiology, environmental health sciences, administration, behavioral
science, and the biological basis of disease. A practice experience
and a capstone experience are also required of all professional
degree students. Master's degrees offered by the school may be
earned on a full- or part-time basis. In addition, the school
participates in a number of combined degree programs with other
schools within the university that lead to the award of a graduate
public health degree along with another professional or undergraduate degree.

COURSE HIGHLIGHTS: Disease Control in Developing Countries/Health Advocacy: Communication and Mobilization/ Community Nutrition/Fate of Toxic Material in the Environment/ Violence Antecedents, Consequences, and Prevention.

SELECTED FACULTY

A.J. Englande: Industrial waste management, wastewater and water treatment, bioremediation, sustainable methods of remediation/treatment.

M. Mahmud Khan: Food security, health economics, health care financing.

Marian McDonald: Women's health, Latino health, community empowerment.

Leslie Snider: Public psychiatry — world trends and current systems of care, cross-cultural psychiatry, mental health and medical anthropology.

SOCIOLOGY

Binghamton University
Department of Sociology
PO Box 6000
Binghamton, NY 13902-6000
Phone (undergraduate): 607-777-2628
Phone (graduate): 607-777-2216
Fax: 607-777-4197
Email: *society@binghamton.edu*
Web site: *sociology.binghamton.edu*
Degrees: B.A., M.A., Ph.D.

At Binghamton University (formerly SUNY-Binghamton), the Department of Sociology's Ph.D. program focuses on the study of long-term, large-scale social change and the historical construction of race, class, and gender. The faculty pursues these issues through new approaches within the historical social sciences. Scholarly development as a researcher and teacher is stressed, rather than standardized training in established specializations. Students in consultation with faculty select their own major fields, design their programs of study, and outline their areas of examination in a rigorous but rewarding environment of coursework in introductory and advanced seminars. (The program may vary depending on student's background and academic progress.)

Following coursework, students continue their program of study through area paper and dissertation seminars. Beyond work in the department, individual programs of study may also include all of the coursework that is desirable in other departments, programs, or schools. Well-prepared students working full time (including summer) on their doctoral studies and research should be able to complete their graduate work in five to six years. Those entering the program with advanced standing can anticipate completion in four to five years. Advanced graduate students often have the opportunity to design and teach undergraduate courses in their major fields. They are also encouraged to participate in the research working groups and other activities of the Fernand Braudel Center.

At the undergraduate level, the curriculum emphasizes two broad areas: the development of world social relations and the development of US social relations, social movements, and social thought. Both stress broad social change processes. Sociology combines readily with racial, ethnic, area, and women's studies, as well as other interdisciplinary social sciences.

COURSE HIGHLIGHTS: Identity, Violence, and Empowerment/ Anti-Systemic Movements/Labor Movements and Social Policy/ Structural Trends in Capitalist World Economy/Modern and Urban Experience in Periphery/Globalization of American Culture.

SELECTED FACULTY

Caglar Keyder: Middle East, Ottoman Empire, development and political economy, world-system, law and the state.
William Martin: Africa, anti-systemic movements, race in global perspectives.
Martin Murray: South Africa and Vietnam, urban-industrial, methods, labor and class analysis, theories.
Benita Roth: US social movements and activism; race, class, and gender; women and work; ethnographic methods.
Kelvin Santiago-Valles: The Caribbean and the US; world-historical critiques of coloniality, political economy, race, and gender; history of knowledges.

Boston College
Department of Sociology
426 McGuinn Hall
Chestnut Hill, MA 02467-3807
Phone: 617-552-4130
Fax: 617-552-4283
Email: *sociolog@bc.edu*
Web site: *www.bc.edu/bc_org/avp/cas/soc/socdept.html*
Degrees: B.A., M.A., Ph.D.

The Sociology Department at Boston College offers Master's and Ph.D. degrees in addition to the B.A. The graduate program, entitled Social Economy and Social Justice: Studies in Race, Class, and Gender, provides a strong background in conceptual and analytical skills and training in a wide variety of applied substantive fields. These include political sociology and social movements; social change and policy planning; criminology, deviance and social control; race and ethnic relations; social psychology; community and family; social stratification; religion and society; sociology of art and popular culture; medical sociology; complex organizations; and social problems of the economy. While graduate students can pursue research in all areas of sociology, the tilt of both faculty and graduate student interest stands at the intersection of social analysis and social change.

COURSE HIGHLIGHTS: Work, Health, and Community/
Sociology of International Migration/Studies in Crime and Social
Justice/Political Economy of World Systems/Sociology of the
Third World/History and Development of Racism/Gender Theory.

SELECTED FACULTY

Severyn Bruyn: Community development, social economy,
cultural evolution.
Charles Derber: Politics and social economy, sociology of
militarism and social change.
Ramón Grosfoguel: Political economy of the capitalist world
system, coloniality, global culture, race and ethnicity, global
cities and international migration.
Stephen Pfohl: Social theory, cultural studies, crime and social
justice, critical perspectives on deviance and social control,
women's studies, sociology of gender.
Eve Spangler: Work and inequality, occupational health
and safety.

University of California, Santa Cruz

Department of Sociology
235 College Eight
Santa Cruz, CA 95064
Phone: 831-459-4306
Email (undergraduate): *hagler@zzyx.ucsc.edu*
Email (graduate): *socyga@cats.ucsc.edu*
Web site: *sociology.ucsc.edu*
Degrees: B.A., Ph.D.

The graduate program in sociology at UC-Santa Cruz leads to the
Ph.D.; an M.A. may be taken en route to the doctorate, but a master's program per se is not available. The core curriculum provides
basic grounding in theory and methods and exposure to research in

three cluster areas of concentration: economy, development, and environment; inequality and identity; and culture, knowledge, and power. Students are expected to specialize in a particular area and take additional coursework offered in that cluster. The program encourages independent, interdisciplinary work, teaching experience, and academic writing skills. Faculty members are presently working in the following areas: political sociology, social inequality, social psychology, feminist theory and the sociology of gender, deviance, race and ethnicity, social movements, sociology of medicine, political economy and economic sociology, historical and comparative analysis, capitalism and nature, language and social interaction, development and underdevelopment in the Third World, culture and mass media, and law and crime.

Sociology majors must complete a total of thirteen courses: three preparatory, four core courses in theory and methods, and six upper division, including at least one in each of the three undergraduate specializations of institutional analysis, social psychology, and inequality and social change. Prior to graduation, sociology majors must also fulfill a comprehensive requirement, which may be either a comprehensive exam, a senior honors thesis, or a score at the fiftieth percentile or better on the GRE Sociology Advanced Test.

COURSE HIGHLIGHTS: Global Corporations and National States/Nature, Poverty, and Progress/Sociology and Social Justice/Hunger and Famine/Political Economy for Sociologists/ Race, Crime, and Justice/Cross-National and Cross-Cultural Research.

SELECTED FACULTY

John Brown Childs: Sociology of knowledge, religion and social action, elitist and populist social movements, ethnicity, race, nationalism, global community.
Ben Crow: Comparative sociology of development; poverty, class, and gender; water, land, and labor; political economy; social studies of technology; peasant studies.

Melanie DuPuis: Economic sociology, sociology of development, political sociology, sociology of the environment, technological change, historical sociology, social theory.

Walter Goldfrank: Global political economy, social movements and revolutions, export agriculture and its impacts, social change, world systems.

Emory University
Department of Sociology
225 Tarbutton Hall
1555 Pierce Drive
Atlanta, GA 30322
Phone: 404-727-7510
Fax: 404-727-7532
Email (graduate): *cdavid@emory.edu*
Email (undergraduate): *doutlaw@emory.edu*
Web site: *www.emory.edu/soc/index.html*
Degrees: B.A., M.A., Ph.D.

The graduate program in the Department of Sociology at Emory University provides rigorous training in theory, research design, and statistics, along with extensive preparation in the following major substantive areas: comparative political economy and development, stratification and organization, social psychology, and culture. The Ph.D. program requires 72 hours of coursework, an M.A. paper, two written examinations (one in a general field and the other in a special field designed by the student), and a dissertation. Ph.D. candidates must also present a paper at professional meetings. The program is designed for completion in five to six years. Almost all graduate students in the Department receive full funding for four years, which typically includes a tuition waiver and combined assistantship and fellowship funding.

Nine sociology courses, or 36 credit hours, are required for the undergraduate major. A combined B.A./M.A. degree is available, as is a stringent honors option involving graduate seminar attendance, completion of a research paper, and a written and/or oral examination. The faculty boasts particular expertise in the comparative study of economic and political trends, in criminology, in health and illness, in social psychology, in the study of culture, and in theories and methods that are central to the discipline.

COURSE HIGHLIGHTS: Political Economy of World Systems/ Women and Development/Mass Media and Social Influence/ Making Sense of Globalization/Race, Gender, and Economic Inequality in the US/Global Structures and Processes.

SELECTED FACULTY

John Boli: World culture and international organizations since 1850, transnational corporations in world-cultural context since 1970, structure and process in the world polity, citizenship and civil society.

Terry Boswell: Work and industry, world system studies, revolutions, historical comparison of ethnic split labor markets, global hegemony since 1496.

Lane Kenworthy: Economic sociology; stratification; political sociology; effects of income inequality, corporatism, and the welfare state on economic performance; gender inequality in politics and the labor market.

Richard Rubinson: Political economy of development, political sociology, sociology of education, organizations.

University of Oregon
Department of Sociology
1291 University of Oregon
Eugene, OR 97403-1291
Phone: 541-346-5002
Fax: 541-346-5026
Email: *sociology@oregon.uoregon.edu*
Web site: *darkwing.uoregon.edu/~sociology/*
Degrees: B.A., M.A., Ph.D.

The graduate program in sociology at the University of Oregon is designed both to give students a thorough grounding in the basic theoretical perspectives and research tools of the discipline and to permit them to achieve special competence in individually selected fields within the discipline. The program leading up to the master's degree concentrates on helping each individual student develop her or his own mastery of theory and methods and of two or more specialty areas within the field. Students admitted to the graduate program with a bachelor's degree will be required to complete 75 credit hours of graduate-level (500 to 600) work for the Ph.D. and 60 such units for an M.A.; most graduate courses are five credit hours. Students must take four substantive graduate seminars or three substantive seminars and a second advanced theory course. Upon completion of the M.A., those wishing to pursue the doctoral program must pass the departmental qualifying examination in theory and methods and two area comprehensive examinations.

Majors in sociology are required to complete a minimum of 44 credit hours of undergraduate sociology courses. The honors program involves an honors seminar and thesis. Concentrations are optional, but among those offered are environment, population, and society; international systems; race, ethnicity, and social change; work, labor, and economy; and politics and social movements.

COURSE HIGHLIGHTS: Workers and Consumers in the Global Economy/Topics in Environmental Sustainability/Crime and Social Control/Urbanization and the City/Systems of War and Peace/Marxist Sociological Theory.

SELECTED FACULTY

Val Burris: Power structure research, corporate and political elites, right-wing movements, politics of the middle classes, methods of social network analysis.
John Bellamy Foster: Ecological crisis, economic crisis, imperialism, social theory.
Linda Fuller: Developing countries, comparative socialism, politics of work and production, social change.

Gregory McLauchlan: Relationships between states, military structures, and social systems; war, peace, and international security; community economic development.
Sandra Morgen: Women and health; race, class, and gender; social movements.

State University of New York, Stony Brook

Department of Sociology
Stony Brook, New York 11794-4356
Phone: 631-632-7700
Fax: 631-632-8203
Email (undergraduate): *sworksman@notes.cc.sunysb.edu*
Email (graduate): *wolivera@notes.cc.sunysb.edu*
Web site: *www.sunysb.edu/sociology/main.html*
Degrees: B.A., M.A., Ph.D.

The Department of Sociology at State University of New York, Stony Brook provides graduate training in sociology informed by a global perspective. Faculty research projects, conferences, and colloquia sponsored by the department provide numerous opportunities for students to actively engage in research, dialogues, and debates relevant to the study of social systems in a world characterized by increasing global interaction. Other fields of expertise include social psychology, cultural sociology, organizations, demography, education, historical sociology, sociology of gender, and science and technology. The department offers both a one-year terminal M.A. and the Ph.D. Master's students are required to complete a thesis. Ph.D. candidates must fulfill residency, coursework, and teaching requirements; complete a professional competence option (either a comprehensive exam and research report, or a series of three papers); and pass an oral preliminary examination before proceeding to the dissertation.

Undergraduate majors must take required and elective courses in sociology and at least three courses in a related field of social science. They must also fulfill an upper-division writing requirement. Acceptance into the honors program depends on approval by the department of a written proposal for a major paper or research project to be completed during the senior year.

COURSE HIGHLIGHTS: Comparative Stratification/Development of Capitalism/Social Movements and Collective Behavior/State and Society in the Middle East/Citizenship and Immigration/ Practice of Ethnography/Global Sociology.

SELECTED FACULTY
Javier Auyero: Sociology of culture, urban poverty and social inequality, Latin American studies, social and cultural theory.
Nilufer Isvan: Rural sociology, comparative sociology, gender, social change.
Timothy Patrick Moran: Comparative sociology; global inequality; sociology of development; stratification—race, class, and gender; quantitative methods.
Michael Schwartz: Economic, historical, and political sociology; Marxist sociology; ethnic relations; social movements.

Also recommended

University of California, Berkeley
Department of Sociology
410 Barrows Hall
Berkeley, CA 94720-1980
Phone: 510-642-4766
Web site: *sociology.berkeley.edu*
Degrees: B.A., M.A., Ph.D.

FACULTY STRENGTHS: Informational society, working families, new markets, labor and women's movements, social mobility, development, affirmative action, schooling, urban gangs, prisons, and churches.

University of California, Davis

Department of Sociology
1282 Social Sciences and Humanities Building
Davis, CA 95616
Phone: 530-752-0782
Fax: 530-752-0783
Web site: *sociology.ucdavis.edu*
Degrees: B.A, M.A., Ph.D.

GRADUATE FIELDS OF STUDY: Collective Behavior–Social
Movements/ Comparative–Historical/Culture/Gender/
Development/Economic Sociology/Law, Deviance, and Social
Control/Methodology/Qualitative and Quantitative/Political
Sociology/Social Psychology (Interaction–Relationships)/
Community and Urban Sociology.

GRADUATE DESIGNATED EMPHASIS SPECIALIZATIONS:
Critical Theory/Economy, Justice, and Society/Feminist Theory
and Research/Native American Studies/Social Theory and
Comparative History.

University of California, Santa Barbara

Department of Sociology
Ellison Hall, Room 2834
Santa Barbara, CA 93106-9430
Phone: 805-893-3118
Web site: *www.soc.ucsb.edu*
Degrees: B.A., M.A., Ph.D.

FACULTY STRENGTHS: Economy and society, ethnomethodology
and conversation analysis, feminist studies, global studies, race
and ethnicity, sociology of culture, social movements,
organizations, stratification, political sociology, urban sociology,
law and social control, religion and society, population and
environment, networks, quantitative and qualitative methods,
sociological theory.

University of Wisconsin, Madison
8128 Social Science Building
1180 Observatory Drive
Madison, WI 53706-1393
Phone: 608-262-2921
Web site: *www.ssc.wisc.edu/soc*
Degrees: B.A., M.A., Ph.D.

GRADUATE FIELDS OF STUDY: Class Analysis and Historical
Change/Communities and Urban Sociology/Demography and
Ecology/Sociology of Deviance, Law, and Social Control/
Economic Sociology/Environmental and Resource Sociology/
Methods and Statistics/Organizational and Occupational
Analysis/Political Sociology/Race and Ethnic Studies/Social
Movements and Collective Action/Social Psychology/Social
Stratification/Sociology of Agriculture/Sociology of Economic
Change/Sociology of Education/Sociology of the Family/
Sociology of Gender/Sociology of Law and Society/Sociology
of Science/General Social Theory.

URBAN AND COMMUNITY PLANNING

University of California, Los Angeles
Department of Urban Planning
3250 Public Policy Building
Box 951656
Los Angeles, CA 90095-1656
Phone: 310-825-4025
Fax: 310-206-5566

Web site: *www.sppsr.ucla.edu/dup*
Degrees: M.A., Ph.D.

Established in 1969, UCLA's Department of Urban Planning has consistently been ranked among the nation's top programs in the field. The department offers both a Master of Arts and a Ph.D. in urban planning. Students in the M.A. program are expected to select one of the following areas of concentration by the end of their first term: regional and international development, social policy and analysis, environmental analysis and policy, and community development and the built environment. In partial fulfillment of the requirements for the master's degree, students are required in the second year to complete either a thesis or one of two comprehensive examination plans: a client project or the two-week examination. The Ph.D. program prepares students for careers in academia as well as for research and policy-making positions in governments and international agencies. A Ph.D. track in regional political economy is offered jointly by the Department of Geography and the Department of Urban Planning.

The department hosts one of the largest clusters of policy specialists on the UCLA campus, and faculty research has had a major impact on planning and public policy on every level, from local community development to the problems of rural development and environmental degradation in the Third World. The university is home to a number of research institutes concerned with issues of planning and policy; graduate students may assist with research, outreach, and technical assistance projects through these organizations.

COURSE HIGHLIGHTS: Urban Housing and Community Development/Political Economy of Urbanization/The Regional World: Territorial Development in a Global Economy/Women and Community Development/Transportation, Land Use, and Urban Form.

SELECTED FACULTY

Leland Burns: Policy and economics of housing.

J. Eugene Grigsby: Urban housing, land use, and economic development strategies.

Susanna Hecht: Political economy of tropical development.

Barbara Nelson: Social and economic policies of industrialized nations, organizational theory and behavior, social movements.

Edward Soja: Urban political economy, planning theory.

Columbia University
Graduate Program in Urban Planning
Graduate School of Architecture, Planning, and Preservation
400 Avery Hall
1172 Amsterdam Avenue
New York, NY 10027
Phone: 212-854-3513
Email: *urbanplanning@columbia.edu*
Web site: *www.arch.columbia.edu/up*
Degrees: M.S., Ph.D.

At Columbia University, the Master of Science program in urban planning emphasizes comparative urbanization and physical and social planning in very large cities. Housing, urban land markets, planning law, and environmental planning are among the major subjects covered. Grounded in an experiential approach, program requirements include a workshop in planning skills, a planning studio, courses in analytic methods, and in planning theory and practice. M.S. candidates complete coursework in core, elective, and area specialization classes (housing, international comparative planning, physical planning and infrastructure development, or urban economic development) and write a master's thesis. The program's Urban Technical Assistance Project, located in West Harlem, provides off-campus space for staff and graduate student interns to conduct planning projects.

A doctoral program in urban planning is also available, and undergraduate students may major in urban studies.

COURSE HIGHLIGHTS: New Patterns of Metropolitan Development/Privatization and the Public Sector/National Housing Policy/Land Use Planning/Sustainable Development and Urbanization/Dimensions of Power and Space/Urban Labor Markets.

SELECTED FACULTY
Sigurd Grava: Physical planning, infrastructure, urban transportation.
Peter Marcuse: Comparative housing and planning policy, effects of globalization on urban social patterns, the interrelation of race, class, and space.
Lionel McIntyre: Community development, housing.
Elliot D. Sclar: Economics of privatization, environmental aspects of planning.

Cornell University
Department of City and Regional Planning
106 West Sibley Hall
Ithaca, NY 14850
Phone: 607-255-4331
Fax: 607-255-1971
Email: *crp_admissions@cornell.edu*
Web site: *www.crp.cornell.edu*
Degrees: B.S., M.R.P., M.A., M.S., Ph.D.

The Department of City and Regional Planning (CRP) at Cornell affords students access to a wide range of scholarly resources. Advanced degrees are available in regional science, history of architecture and urbanism, professional studies in international development, and historic preservation planning, in addition to city and regional planning. Graduate degrees are offered at both the master's and Ph.D. levels. These programs provide both professional education in the various branches of the planning field and advanced, specialized education for those who seek careers in teaching, research, and policymaking. In the Master's of Regional Planning program, concentrations are available in land use and environmental planning, economic development planning: communities and regions, and international studies in planning. At the doctoral level, students may concentrate on city and regional planning, planning theory and systems analysis, regional science, urban and regional theory, and urban planning history.

The CRP offers a Bachelor of Science degree in urban and regional studies. In addition to satisfying college-wide distribution requirements, students take five core courses, eleven area courses (at least one each from the CRP sub-fields of design, economics, environment, history, quantitative analysis, and politics and policy), and six to nine CRP electives.

COURSE HIGHLIGHTS: Pre-Industrial Cities and Towns of North America/Urban Housing: Sheltered versus Unsheltered Society/Urban Archaeology/Industrial Restructuring: Implications for State and Local Policy/Gender Issues in Planning and Architecture.

SELECTED FACULTY

Lourdes Benería: Labor markets, women's work, gender and development, globalization, European integration, Latin American development.

William W. Goldsmith: US urban policy, development and underdevelopment.

David B. Lewis: Science and technology policy in developing nations, rural development.

Barbara Lynch: International environmental issues, natural resource and rural development policy, nongovernmental organizations as political actors.

Porus Olpadwala: Comparative international development, international urbanization, technology development and transfer, transnational corporations.

University of Massachusetts, Lowell

Department of Regional Economic and Social Development
61 Wilder Street
Lowell, MA 01854
Phone: 978-934-2900
Email: *resd@uml.edu*
Web site: *www.uml.edu/Dept/RESD*
Degrees: M.A.

Formed in 1997, the Department of Regional Economic and Social Development at the University of Massachusetts at Lowell unites development theories with practice by integrating classroom learning with regional, national, and international social development projects and research in which the faculty are engaged. Candidates for the Master of Arts degree focus on one of three areas of concentration: regional and community development; organization, technology, and policy; and social and historical dynamics of development. Graduate students may be enrolled full- or part-time; all core courses and certain electives are offered during evening hours.

The department does not currently grant an undergraduate major, but several undergraduate courses are taught, and juniors and seniors are eligible to apply for a joint B.A./M.A. degree program.

COURSE HIGHLIGHTS: Island Economies/Production and Sustainable Development/Comparative Industrial Revolutions/ Municipal Management/Community-Based Planning/ Development and International Competition/Work, Technology, and Training.

SELECTED FACULTY

Laurence Gross: 19th- and 20th-century labor, technology, and industrialization.

William Mass: Technological and organizational change, comparative industrial development, local and regional development policies.

Linda Silka: Community capacity building, refugee and immigrant leadership, community-university partnerships, community conflict resolution.
Chris Tilly: Economic restructuring, low wage jobs, poverty and inequality, community and regional development.

Southern New Hampshire University

Community Economic Development Program
Graduate School of Business
2500 North River Road
Manchester, NH 03106-1045
Phone: 603-644-3103
Fax: 603-644-3130
Email: *karim@minerva.nhc.edu*
Web site: *merlin.nhc.edu*
Degrees: M.S., Ph.D.

Southern New Hampshire University's Community Economic Development (CED) program provides technical skills in finance, management, legal structures, organizational systems, land use, cooperatives, and housing and business development to people working with community-based agencies and to groups representing the interests of low-income people in urban and rural settings. Part of the university's Graduate School of Business, the program promotes the view of community development as a strategy combining social and economic activities that facilitate total community benefit rather than individual financial gain.

North American students may earn a master's degree in community economic development through the University's weekend program, which requires attendance at the school one weekend per month, Friday to Sunday, for 17 months. The CED program offers a Ph.D. degree in both residential and weekend formats. The doctorate is designed for the practitioner who wishes to pursue research and a teaching career. Affiliated with the CED program are four training institutes and partnerships with local nonprofits.

COURSE HIGHLIGHTS: Organizational Management for
Community Organizations/Business Development/Diversity in
Organizations/Housing and Land Policy/Indigenous Economics/
Law and Community Development/Community Organizing.

SELECTED FACULTY

Clark Arrington: Employee-owned cooperative corporations,
nonprofit corporations, business finance.
Chris Clamp: Cooperatives, training of trainers, curriculum
development, women's economic development.
Marcy Goldstein-Gelb: International and domestic
microenterprise.
Peter Uvin: Structural adjustment; food aid; institution building;
local government in Africa; programming, monitoring and
evaluation of assistance.

University of New Mexico
Community and Regional Planning Program
2414 Central SE
Albuquerque, New Mexico 87106
Phone: 505-277-5050
Email: *crp@unm.edu*
Web site: *saap.unm.edu*
Degree: M.C.R.P.

The mission of the Masters in Community and Regional Planning
(M.C.R.P.) program at the University of New Mexico is to plan and
advocate for sustainable communities and ecosystems within the
Southwest region through education, service, and research.
Students of the M.C.R.P. program learn to create community-based
plans and programs that sustain and enhance a community's
culture, resource base, built environment, and economic vitality.
Along with public forums and lecture series, the CRP program has
established a Design Planning and Assistance Center through which
faculty and students provide planning and design services to
hundreds of clients across the state, including low-income individ-

uals and families, neighborhood associations, citizens' groups, cooperatives, rural communities, and public agencies.

The master's program requires a minimum of 50 credit hours of study. Students must also complete a thesis or professional project. The CRP curriculum includes numerous undergraduate planning courses, and a Bachelor of Arts in environmental design is available. The program also offers dual degrees in planning and Latin American studies, public administration, and public health.

COURSE HIGHLIGHTS: Political Economy of Urban Development/ Cultural Aspects of Community Development/Watershed Management/Natural Resource Economics/Advanced Site and Environment/Planning Process and Issues of Native American Reservations.

SELECTED FACULTY

Teresa Córdova: Community development, urban Latinos, political economy.

David Henkel: Transnational resource management, development and regional planning.

Claudia Isaac: Planning theory, Latin American planning, gender and development.

Theodore S. Jojola: Indigenous human rights, indigenous planning, tribal economic development.

Paul Lusk: Appropriate technology, rural planning, physical and land use planning.

Pratt Institute
Graduate Center for Planning and the Environment
200 Willoughby Avenue
Brooklyn, NY 11205
Phone: 718-399-4314
Fax: 718-399-4332
Email: *info@pratt.edu*
Web site: *www.pratt.edu/arch/gcpe*
Degree: M.S.

Pratt Institute's Graduate Center for Planning and the Environment (GCPE) is a unit of its School of Architecture. The GCPE is a leading international center for the study of community-based and participatory planning. The courses are offered primarily in the evening and on weekends at Pratt's Brooklyn and Manhattan campuses, giving students maximum flexibility to work full-time in a variety of public, private, or nonprofit agencies. The structure of the programs makes it possible to draw faculty from a wide pool of practicing professionals throughout the New York area, contributing to the GCPE's strong emphasis on work-related skills. In keeping with its flexible, interdisciplinary approach, the Graduate Center for Planning and the Environment welcomes applicants with undergraduate degrees in a wide range of academic disciplines.

The Center offers two degree programs: a 63-credit Master of Science in city and regional planning and a 40-credit Master of Science in environmental planning. It also has a combined program in architecture and planning for undergraduate architecture students and a joint degree program in planning and law in conjunction with Brooklyn Law School.

COURSE HIGHLIGHTS: Planning for Sustainable Communities/ Advocacy Planning–Social Action/Urbanization in Developing Nations/Neighborhood Commercial Revitalization/Waste Management and Remediation/Tourism and Historic Preservation.

SELECTED FACULTY

Tom Angotti: Community development, environmental issues.
Eva Hanhardt: Planning and the environment.
William Menking: Architecture, built environment.
Ronald Shiffman: Brownfield revitalization, advocacy planning.

WOMEN'S STUDIES

University of Arizona
Women's Studies Department
Communication Building 108
PO Box 210025
Tucson, AZ 85721-0025
Phone: 520-621-7338
Fax: 520-621-1533
Email: *lbernal@u.arizona.edu*
Web site: *w3.arizona.edu/~ws/*
Degrees: B.A., M.A.

The Women's Studies Department Master of Arts program at the University of Arizona offers students the opportunity to develop their understanding and analyses of feminist thought and movements in an interdisciplinary atmosphere. Adjunct professors in outside departments broaden and complement the teaching of the women's studies faculty. Students are encouraged to undertake internship opportunities and may, with guidance from their committees, write an M.A. project that builds upon their internship. The program prepares students for both doctoral work and a career addressing feminist concerns. Requirements for the degree include 36 total units of coursework (at least 21 in women's studies), an M.A. project, and an oral exam and presentation of the M.A. project. Students are also expected to attend women's studies colloquia. The undergraduate program encourages community interaction and independent study and emphasizes strong written and oral communication skills, group work, and technology-based research. A portfolio of papers is required.

Women's studies' internationally prestigious research division, the Southwest Institute for Research on Women (SIROW), was created in 1979. SIROW develops collaborative research projects, particularly on women in the Southwest and US-Mexican border region; links researchers, community organizations, and policy makers; and supports education about and for women and girls.

COURSE HIGHLIGHTS: Gender, Difference, and Power: Postcolonial Studies and Race Theory/Cultures of Biology, Medicine, Gender, and Race/Women's Activisms and Organizations/Women in International Development/Feminist and IR Theories/Feminist Ethics.

SELECTED FACULTY

Laura Briggs: US women's history, social and cultural studies of science, critical race theory, postcolonial studies.
Elisabeth Clemens: Interaction of social movements and formal political institutions in processes of institutional change.
Miranda Joseph: Cultural studies, Marx and Marxisms, queer theory.
Patricia MacCorquodale: Sexuality; women and girls in science and math; gender in educational, employment and family settings; intersections of gender and ethnicity.

University of California, Riverside
Women's Studies Department
Riverside, CA 92521
Phone: 909-787-6427
Fax: 909-787-6386
Email: *christine.gailey@ucr.edu*
Web site: *www.ucr.edu/chss/depts/womstu/womenhome.html*
Degree: B.A.

The Women's Studies Department at the University of California, Riverside combines theory with informed action and focuses on understanding varieties of feminism throughout the world today. The curriculum crosses traditional academic disciplines to investigate such topics as the roles of women in developing countries and in migration; the ways gender interacts with race, ethnicity, and class; the functions of gender categories in our own and other societies; history and contemporary theory of sex and sexuality; and new directions in feminist theory and methods of research. Faculty affiliated with Women in Coalition (WIC), the research arm of the department, conduct research that involves collaboration with grassroots women's organizations in the US and other countries. WIC also organizes conferences and brings women scholar-activists from around the world to speak on campus.

Over thirty full-time faculty regularly teach courses in women's studies or cross-list their courses with women's studies. Students may receive academic credit for working with community organizations. The university's honors program offers special courses for honors undergraduates.

COURSE HIGHLIGHTS: Issues in Feminisms, Representation, and Ethnographic Practice/Gender, Kinship, and Social Change/ Women's Labor and the Economy/Women of Early Christianity/ Gender and Development in Latin America and the Caribbean.

SELECTED FACULTY

Amalia Cabezas: Comparative sexuality, sex tourism, women's health in international perspective, gender in Latin America.
Piya Chatterjee: Historical anthropology of colonialism, cultural analysis of pedagogy, nongovernmental organizing, Third World feminist theory and politics.
Christine Ward Gailey: Gender hierarchies under conditions of domination, gender and state formation, colonialism and gender, feminist methodologies, gendered violence and family formation, grassroots women's responses to development agendas.

Minnesota State University, Mankato
Women's Studies Department
Morris Hall 109
Mankato, MN 56001
Phone: 507-389-2077
Fax: 507-389-6377

Email: *cynthia.veldhuisen@mnsu.edu*
Web site: *www.mnsu.edu/womenst/*
Degrees: B.A., B.S., M.S.

The Master of Science in Women's Studies at Minnesota State University, Mankato is an internationally known program that attracts students from throughout the US and abroad. Based predominantly in the social sciences, the graduate program combines coursework, internships, cross-disciplinary seminars, and individual and cooperative research projects in a decidedly feminist comprehensive program. It is oriented toward training activists who wish to promote social change in a variety of settings, including feminist and women-oriented centers and organizations, academia, and government. Students may combine interests in such areas as counseling, public policy, feminist research, community action, cultural work, or teaching with feminist theory, methodology, and knowledge.

The department supports a variety of social and educational opportunities, including organizations, forums, workshops, socials, and research projects. Students are encouraged to take leadership roles in the development of special programs and to become actively involved with community organizations and with related campus groups.

COURSE HIGHLIGHTS: Feminist Jurisprudence–Women and the Law/Women, Poverty, and Welfare/Women, Work, and the Environment/Global Feminisms/Rural Women/Women, Sex, and Identity/Collective Action and Analysis/Feminist Pedagogy.

SELECTED FACULTY

Maria Bevacqua: Women and law, feminist theories, research methods, rape theories.
Donna Langston: Feminist theory, lesbian studies, race and class issues, history of second wave feminism.
Carol Perkins: Feminist theory, history, and education.

Oberlin College

Women's Studies Program
10 North Professor Street
Rice Hall 116
Oberlin, OH 44074
Phone: 440-775-8907
Fax: 440-775-6698
Email: *linda.pardee@oberlin.edu*
Web site: *www.oberlin.edu/~wstudies*
Degree: B.A.

Women's Studies at Oberlin College is an interdisciplinary program focusing on feminist analyses of the ways in which gender, sexuality, race, class, and nationality inform women's lives. Coursework examines scholarship by and about women in different historical eras and geographical regions; the curriculum emphasizes women's movements, agency, and forms of resistance at the analytical and practical levels. Women's studies classes investigate materials previously neglected by scholars, develop methodological and critical approaches to materials customarily treated in other ways, and propose revisions in the content, methods, and assumptions of particular disciplines in light of recent feminist scholarship.

The women's studies major consists of a minimum of 30 credits of course work, with nine credits maximum at the introductory level. A practicum consisting of volunteer work with a feminist or social justice organization is also required. Senior women's studies majors may conduct independent, original research under the supervision of an advisor, normally drawn from the women's studies program committee. Students are expected to prepare a substantive project or research paper and pass an oral examination on their research and its relationship to relevant bodies of feminist scholarship.

COURSE HIGHLIGHTS: Gender, Social Change, and Social Movements/Women, Work, and the Persistence of Inequality/

The American Family: Comfort, Conflict, and Criticism/Gender and the State in the Middle East/Feminist Religious Thought in Multicultural Perspective.

SELECTED FACULTY

Frances Hasso: Gender, race/nation, post-coloniality, identity, inequality, social movements, epistemology, gender and nationalism in the Middle East.
Wendy Kozol: Cultural politics of gender, feminist theory, and feminist methodologies; American women, families, and popular culture.
Sonia Kruks: Political theory from ancient times to the present, feminist political thought, theories of social power.

University of Washington
Department of Women Studies
B110 Padelford, Box 354345
Seattle, WA 98195-4345
Phone: 206-543-6900
Fax: 206-685-9555
Email: *clangdon@u.washington.edu*
Web site: *depts.washington.edu/webwomen/*
Degrees: B.A., M.A., Ph.D.

Initiated in 1997, the graduate program in women studies at the University of Washington is the first of its kind in the Northwest. Based in research with a critical, theoretical, social science orientation, the women studies program at the University of Washington provides a cohesive framework for the study of women's and men's lives within historical and contemporary contexts and from multidisciplinary and multicultural perspectives. The department encourages students to learn actively through community internships and by developing feminist theories and methods that contribute to the ongoing movements for social change around the world.

The M.A. and Ph.D. programs prepare students for careers in both academia and other professions, especially in the nonprofit sector. Ph.D. students must exhibit proficiency in a language rele-vant to their theoretical and/or regional areas of specialization. Students are urged to establish foreign language competence before entering the graduate school or as early as possible in their graduate careers. At the undergraduate level, several major tracks are available, including women and law; women and health; women and social change; and race, ethnicity, and gender. A senior thesis is required.

COURSE HIGHLIGHTS: Gender and Globalization: Theory and Process/Comparative Women's Movements and Activism/ Feminism, the State, and Democracy in Indonesia/Ideologies and Technologies of Motherhood: Race, Class, and Sexuality/ Economics of Gender.

SELECTED FACULTY
Tani Barlow: Modern Chinese gender history, international feminism.
Susan Jeffords: Feminist theory, gender and militarism issues.
Priti Ramamurthy: Political economy of development, transnational feminism, irrigation, agro-food systems, South Asia.
Shirley Yee: US women's history, African American women's history, the intersection of race and gender in US social reform movements.

INDEX

ABOUT FOOD FIRST
(Institute for Food and Development Policy)

Food First, also known as the Institute for Food and Development Policy, is a nonprofit research and education-for-action center dedicated to exposing the root causes of hunger in a world of plenty. It was founded in 1975 by Frances Moore Lappé, author of the bestseller *Diet for a Small Planet,* and food policy analyst Dr. Joseph Collins. Food First research has revealed that hunger is created by concentrated economic and political power, not by scarcity. Resources and decision-making are in the hands of a wealthy few, depriving the majority of land, jobs, and therefore food.

Hailed by *The New York Times* as "one of the most established food think tanks in the country," Food First has grown to profoundly shape the debate about hunger and development.

But Food First is more than a think tank. Through books, reports, videos, media appearances, and speaking engagements, Food First experts not only reveal the often hidden roots of hunger, they show how individuals can get involved in bringing an end to the problem. Food First inspires action by bringing to light the courageous efforts of people around the world who are creating farming and food systems that truly meet people's needs.

HOW TO BECOME A MEMBER OR INTERN OF FOOD FIRST

BECOME A MEMBER

Private contributions and membership gifts form the financial base of Food First/Institute for Food and Development Policy. The success of the Institute's programs depends not only on its dedicated volunteers and staff, but on financial activists as well. Each member strengthens Food First's efforts to change a hungry world. We invite you to join Food First. As a member you will receive a twenty percent discount on all Food First books. You will also receive our quarterly publication, *Food First News and Views,* and timely *Backgrounders* that provide information and suggestions for action on current food and hunger crises in the United States and around the world. If you want to subscribe to our internet newsletter, *Food Rights Watch,* send us an e-mail at *foodfirst@foodfirst.org.* All contributions are tax-deductible.

BECOME AN INTERN

There are opportunities for interns in research, advocacy, campaigning, publishing, computers, media, and publicity at Food First. Our interns come from around the world. They are a vital part of our organization and make our work possible.

To become a member or apply to become an intern, just call, visit our Web site, or write to us at

>Food First/Institute for Food and Development Policy
>398 60th Street, Oakland, CA 94618, USA
>Phone: (510) 654-4400 Fax: (510) 654-4551
>Email: *foodfirst@foodfirst.org*
>Web site: *www.foodfirst.org*

You are also invited to give a gift membership to others interested in the fight to end hunger.